Further praise for *Ecotherapy: A Field Guide*

This book provides a refreshingly critical view of ecotherapy, seeking to make better sense of this emerging field at a pivotal time in its development. I also love the way it attempts to bridge western and indigenous ways of thinking about nature, which is essential to the healing that industrial growth culture so desperately needs.
Mary-Jayne Rust, art therapist, Jungian analyst and ecopsychotherapist, and author of *Towards an Ecopsychotherapy*

This excellent book by Dave Key and Keith Tudor is as refreshing as it is academically rigorous, documenting some of the entangled epistemological issues within ecotherapy literature alongside contemporary accounts of the ancient hermeneutic practice of deep listening to land. It is an important contribution to the emerging dialogue between deep ecology and indigenous relationships with nature.
Roger Duncan MSc, UKCP, systemic, family and ecopsychotherapist, systemic supervisor and author of *Nature in Mind: Systemic Thinking and Imagination in Ecopsychology and Mental Health*

Forget everything you have ever heard about eco-psychological therapy. This book deftly explores the cultural issues that plague modern ecotherapy, combining old ways of knowing with new ways of practice. This book takes you on a literary journey into meta-theory and the cultural complexities of modern ecotherapy practice, and grapples successfully with issues of cultural appropriation in ecopsychology and therapy. A must read for those struggling with whakapapa, belonging and cultural relevance. This book invites a deeper communion about the nomenclature and reframing of modern ecotherapy. Key and Tudor superbly illustrate the inner whakapapa that exists within culture and ecotherapy. A field guide to belonging, nature, and intimate human relations.
John Perrott (Te Arawa/Pākehā), Associate Head of School, Māori Enhancement, School of Environmental Science, Auckland University of Technology

This timely and exciting book provides an excellent overview and analysis of the field of ecotherapy, comprehensively outlining the territory of diverse contexts, terminology and practices and bringing much-needed cohesion and clarification. With a helpful metatheory which incorporates the different paradigms involved, the authors propose an elegant inclusive way of understanding thorny, ongoing issues and debates. Most pertinently, this thoughtful guide skilfully embodies the principles and paradigm it is espousing, including indigenous voices and poetic expressions that sing to our soul and convey the felt sense and spirit of our connectedness and belonging with "the wild earth that holds and heals us all". Dave Key and Keith Tudor offer a welcome and important contribution to this emergent field so significant for our troubled times.
Tania Dolley, counselling psychologist and ecopsychologist

Accurate, accessible and understands both the subtleties and the gravity of the issues that the ecotherapy world is wrestling with. It offers clarity in a field that can be confusing. I will reference this book in my teaching workshops.
Matthew Henson MSc, UKCP, ICP, existential psychotherapist, ecotherapist, trainer and group facilitator in private practice

Ecotherapy

A Field Guide

Ecotherapy

A Field Guide

David Key and Keith Tudor

First published in 2023 by
Phoenix Publishing House Ltd
62 Bucknell Road
Bicester
Oxfordshire OX26 2DS

10 9 8 7 6 5 4 3 2 1

British Library Cataloguing in Publication Data
A catalogue record for this book is available from the British Library.

ISBN: 978-1-915565-02-0 (paperback)
ISBN: 978-1-915565-03-7 (ebook)

Typeset by Bespoke Publishing Ltd.
Printed in the UK.

www.firingthemind.com

Contents

List of tables

List of figures

About the authors

David Key is an independent ecopsychology consultant specializing in the design and facilitation of outdoor programmes that catalyse and support pro-ecological social change. He holds a Bachelor of Arts degree in Design, a Master's degree in Human Ecology and is an internationally qualified outdoor leader. He led one of the world's first by-prescription ecotherapy programmes and has provided professional development training in the field since 2005. He also has an online coaching practice for individuals who apply ecopsychology in a diversity of contexts. He loves trail running, telemark skiing, tramping (hiking), sailing and sea fishing.

Keith Tudor is professor of psychotherapy at Auckland University of Technology (AUT), where he is also a co-lead of the AUT Group for Research in the Psychological Therapies. A qualified social worker and psychotherapist, he is interested in the social and political context of and on therapeutic practice as well as the impact of therapeutic theory on thinking about the social, political and ecological context. From 2012 to 2022, he was the editor of *Psychotherapy and Politics International* (Wiley/Tuwhera), is the editor of the 'Advancing Theory in Therapy' book series (Routledge) and is the co-author, with Bernie Neville, of *Eco-centred Therapy: Revisioning the Person-centred Approach for a Living World* (Routledge, 2023).

About the contributors

Ben Classen is a PhD student at Victoria University of Wellington. His primary research interests are in discrepancies in perception and behaviour across online/offline contexts. Having recently published work about the contemporary mental health landscape in Aotearoa New Zealand, Ben's work benefits from a broad and interdisciplinary research background.

Dion Enari is a lecturer in the School of Sport and Recreation, Faculty of Health & Environmental Sciences at Auckland University of Technology. He holds a PhD in Samoan culture from Bond University, Gold Coast, Australia and Lefaoali'i (high-talking Chief) title from Lepa, Samoa. His research interests include sport management, sport leadership, mental health, Pacific language, Indigenous studies and trans-nationalism.

Rebecca Freeth is a practitioner and scholar who facilitates, researches, teaches and writes about collaboration. For the last twenty years, she has facilitated dialogue on issues that require taking seriously diverse perspectives and experiences in order to move forward together. In 2019, Rebecca completed her doctoral research on interdisciplinary collaboration in the field of sustainability. She works as a senior consultant with Reos Partners Africa and is an associate scholar with the Institute for Advanced Sustainability Studies in Potsdam, Germany.

Rupert Hutchinson is an international mountain leader, outdoor guide, facilitator and coach based within the Findhorn watershed of north-east Scotland. Together with his partner, he runs an experience-led sustainability consultancy which is a certified B Corp, working with purpose-driven leaders, often outdoors, to catalyse shifts in policy and practice towards a more regenerative future. He loves to hike, ski, cook over campfires and sleep out under the night sky.

Hayley Marshall, MSc, CTA, PTSTA(P), is a UK-based clinical specialist in ecological therapy, having worked outside for over fifteen years. She has written articles and book chapters on outdoor practice. In collaboration with educator Giles Barrow, she has been at the forefront of the recent development of ecological transactional analysis. Hayley is the ecological training consultant for Red Kite Training in Liverpool, UK, and offers a variety of outdoor training courses at The Centre for Natural Reflection.

Jacoba Matapo is an associate professor in the School of Education, Faculty of Culture and Society at Auckland University of Technology. Her research specializes in Indigenous Pacific philosophy and pedagogy in Pacific early childhood education. Her work advocates for the value of Indigenous knowledge systems in education, and the possibilities of transformation through relational ecologies, storytelling and the art of embodied literacies.

Gina Mārie O'Neill is of Ngāti Kahungunu, Rangitane (Aotearoa), Irish and German descent, currently living and working on unceded Gadigal and Bundjalung lands in Australia. She is a registered clinical psychotherapist, Indigenous healing practitioner, educator and consultant supervisor. Gina has worked in private psychiatric clinical settings, public health settings and private practice for over twenty years and, in the last ten years, as a supervisor, lecturer/trainer and Aboriginal health worker. As a Māori woman, Gina's interest is in growing her Indigenous healing practices in reciprocity with the natural world, and in the intersection with Gestalt psychotherapy to support re-connection and healing of the relationships with people, land and spirit.

Bianca Stawiarski operates Indigenous social enterprise Warida Wholistic Wellness, and is an allied health professional specializing in decolonizing mental health on Country, particularly in the area of complex, developmental trauma and culturally informed, trauma – integrated system change approaches. She is a strong Badimaya and Ukrainian woman, who is a centred and purpose-driven healer, consultant, coach, speaker, lecturer, international co-author, trainer and change-maker. As part of her life's work, she is exploring ngardi guwanda, Indigenous healing and lived experiences of dissociative identity disorder.

Acknowledgements

Dave would like to thank Tania Dolley, Hilary Prentice, Brendon Hill and Mary-Jayne Rust for their seminal roles in putting ecopsychology on the map in the UK in the 1990s. He would especially like to thank Mary-Jayne for her professional collaboration and beautiful friendship, which have formed a solid foundation and inspiration for his practice since the mid-2000s. Dave would also like to thank his partner Libby Prenton and his daughter Maia Rose, for supporting his unusual vocation, which has often taken him away from home and which has mostly been a labour of love. Finally, he would like to thank Pam Key, his Mum, for a thousand walks along the edges. Keith would like to acknowledge his parents, Joan Philipson Tudor and Leslie Charles Tudor, for instilling in him a love of mountains and fell walking, specifically in the English Lake District; Hayley Marshall for introducing him to outdoor therapy, and Hayley and Giles Barrow for their work in developing a sensibility in transactional analysis (TA) to EcoTA; tangata whenua (people of the land) here in Aotearoa New Zealand for being precisely people of land and for the teaching and learning that offers; Bernie Neville who, in 2020, joined the family of things; and Esther Tudor for her love of Stella, her canine companion, and for her advocacy of human–canine relationships which he continues to find challenging. Finally, each of us would like to acknowledge our friendship, which has developed, not least through the writing of this book; and both of us would like to thank Angie Strachan for her editorial skills and input; Jane Ryan at Confer, and Christina Wipf Perry, Eva Townsend Bilton and Liz Wilson at Karnac Books; Kate Pearce at Phoenix Publishing House; and, of course, the wild earth that holds and heals us all.

Introduction

This book presents the results of an extensive scoping review of the field of ecotherapy, using a methodology informed by critical theory and deep ecology. Consistent with this, and the fact that our own critical thinking has been informed by contact with Indigenous peoples, especially in our adopted homeland of Aotearoa New Zealand, the results are presented in a way that privileges traditions that predate the modern interest in this subject.

Following a review of the literature, the discussion explores six paired terms derived from a critical analysis of the findings: human and nature; therapy and therapeutic; wilderness and wild; physical and metaphysical; culture and indigeneity; and the 'skin-bound self' and the 'ecological Self'. This exploration unearths many ambiguities in the way ecotherapy is understood and described, which leads to a proposed metatheory for ecotherapy practice that aims to bring some cohesion to the field and support its future development. The conclusion argues that great care should be taken by ecotherapists in how they practise and describe their work, as many of the terms currently being used are culturally inappropriate and therapeutically counterproductive.

The process that led to this book began when the authors came together in 2019 to explore ecopsychology and its practice through ecotherapy and, specifically, how this might impact education/training in psychotherapy. This exploration quickly exposed many limitations within the narrative of these new disciplines, caused primarily by language, but also by a lack of professional cohesion. We discussed ambiguities in concepts such as self, nature, therapy and (psycho)therapist. Issues of otherness, colonization and hegemony also surfaced as two middle-aged, white, well-educated, male émigrés, living in a land with its own Indigenous population and strong cultural identity, wrestled with shame and guilt as well as anger and a heartfelt desire for social justice and change.

After more than a year of dialogue, Keith brought together a small research group at Auckland University of Technology to try and bring some of these narratives together more formally. This group ebbed and flowed until the question at the core of this book, 'How can we make sense of the field of ecotherapy?', finally became clear. We would like to thank the members of that group – Elizabeth Day, Emma Green, Margot Solomon, Alison Strasser and Kerry Thomas-Anttila – for those early discussions and for their initial input into the research (which forms Chapter 2), albeit that we take responsibility for moving the project to completion and for the final content. We would also like to thank Ben Classen for his initial work as a research associate on the project and, therefore, his contribution to Chapter 2. As we wrote and developed the ideas that you read in the book, we wanted to find a way of including others, and so decided to invite some colleagues to read the manuscript and offer their responses to it. The result, together with our reflections on their responses, forms Chapter 5, and we are delighted to thank Dion Enari, Rebecca Freeth, Rupert Hutchinson, Hayley Marshall, Jacoba Matapo, Gina O'Neill and Bianca Stawiarski for their thoughtful and stimulating contributions.

NOTE TO THE READER

The front cover of this book is a picture of a section of the Whanganui River in Aotearoa New Zealand. In 2017, this river was given the same legal rights under New Zealand law as human beings. This is the second time in history, anywhere in the world, that a more-than-human entity has been given equal legal status to human beings under non-customary law. The first time was in 2014 with regard to Te Urewera National Forest, also in Aotearoa New Zealand. Although these rulings constitute a break-through in non-customary law, this status is nothing new to the ancient traditions of many indigenous cultures whose ancestry and identity are synonymous with the more-than-human world, such that there is just the world. It is, of course, somewhat ironic that the highest degree of legal status under Western law is that of human personhood, as it places the entire more-than-human world as secondary, even when exceptions are made. It is also ironic that, in order to have value under Western law, Te Urewera and the Whanganui River must be anthropomorphized. While the legal personification of more-than-human nature is extremely complex, if you travel down the Whanganui River itself, you do not need the law to know its status, a point that is reflected in a whakataukī (Māori proverb): Ko au te awa, ko te awa ko au | I am the river, the river is me. Our thanks go to John Perrott for his cultural advice on this matter.

1.

Scoping review

In this chapter, we set out the method by which we undertook this research and the methodology and underlying theoretical influences that informed it.

Method

In the Introduction, we referred to the fact that this work began in a series of group discussions with colleagues. These discussions and preliminary searches identified a considerable range of discrete terms and practices, that is, ecotherapy, ecopsychology, outdoor therapy and so on. However, the searches quickly revealed that the relationship between these terms was both complex and ambiguous, and so our initial working research question became: 'How can we make sense of the field of ecotherapy?'

As this question involved defining the field, a scoping review was undertaken as a means of mapping the relationships between a wide range of practices and theories related to 'ecotherapy'. Scoping reviews have become increasingly used to map broad areas of research within and across health science disciplines (Pham *et al.*, 2014). The scoping review is a means of providing a broad overview of contemporary perspectives as well as theoretical gaps within a field (Peters *et al.*, 2015), with the potential for this insight to inform further more systematic reviews in the future (Arksey & O'Malley, 2005).

An initial list of 22 keywords was created, along with a broad research question, as is consistent with established methodological frameworks for conducting scoping reviews (Arksey & O'Malley, 2005). Following further discussion, our research question became: 'What is the range of contemporary perspectives on ecologically minded and ecologically informed therapeutic practice, and what theoretical and/or practical relationships exist between these approaches?' This research question was kept intentionally broad in order to keep the review process iterative and responsive to our developing knowledge of the field. Keywords were used to search for peer-reviewed studies and other relevant literature via various public health databases (i.e. PsycINFO, PubMed and Web of Science), along with supplementary searches of more general databases (Google Scholar and Dimensions). Given the large number of distinct terms in our list of keywords, it was decided that the priority for disseminating our search results would be by identifying the most widely cited publications, along with foundational texts for each of the respective search terms. This approach improved our chances of clarifying conceptual and theoretical overlap between as many sub-disciplines as possible, and as such was consistent with the traditional aims of a scoping review (Peterson *et al.*, 2017).

The process of identifying the key literature and delineating and defining search terms was undertaken by Ben Classen, our research assistant (and co-author of Chapter 2), over a period of three months. Notes, sources and data were exchanged within the research team throughout this process, and regular meetings over the same period enabled the group to discuss initial results and to make recommendations regarding search terms. Through this process, two search terms were excluded from the original list ('animal-assisted therapy' and 'equine-assisted therapy'), as they were deemed to be less relevant to the overarching theme of ecotherapy than initially presumed. Similarly, one new keyword occasionally appeared during the preliminary stages of the review and was deemed relevant enough to our research question to warrant being added to the list of search terms ('eco-anxiety'). The complete list of search terms used throughout the scoping review was: 'adventure therapy', 'applied ecopsychology', 'despair and empowerment work', 'eco-anxiety', 'ecopsychology', 'ecopsychotherapy', 'ecotherapy', 'environmental psychology', 'forest bathing', 'Indigenous psychology', 'Indigenous (psycho)therapy', 'nature therapy', 'nature-based therapy', 'outdoor therapy', 'outdoor yoga', 'rites of passage work', 'shamanic practices', 'terrapsychology', 'wild mindfulness' and 'wild therapy'.

Having established search terms and completed the initial scoping work, the two authors took on the completion of the project. We have: reworked and reordered the material (the findings presented in Chapter 2), privileging Indigenous traditions; become much clearer about the methodology underpinning the second phase of the project (see next section); written up and developed the discussion (which forms Chapter 3); and identified and added an analysis (Chapter 4).

We are aware of the exponential growth of this field, and that even our relatively extensive list of search terms is not complete. In the time since the original search was conducted, we have become aware of 'marine therapy' (Soto, 2008), 'green therapy' (Verzwyvelt *et al.*, 2021) and 'blue therapy' (Britton *et al.*, 2018; White *et al.*, 2016), to name just a few. Whilst we acknowledge this, it does not detract from the main purpose of the scoping review; it simply suggests that practitioners, educators and activists need to keep up to date with the field. Nor does it detract from our analysis and the metatheory we propose, within which, we suggest, any addition to or development of the field can be located.

Methodology

Two methodologies inform the way in which we consider the findings of this scoping review: one based on critical theory and specifically post-colonial theory and the other based on deep ecology.

Critical and post-colonial theory

In modern times and in the Western intellectual tradition, critical theory is often associated with the Institute for Social Research at Goethe University, Frankfurt, Germany, more commonly referred to as 'the Frankfurt School'. Founded in 1923 by Carl Grünberg, a Marxist professor of law, the Institute was largely funded by Felix Weil, a wealthy student whose doctoral dissertation had dealt with the practical problems of implementing socialism. The Frankfurt School comprised intellectuals, academics and political dissidents who were dissatisfied with the contemporary socio-economic systems (capitalist, fascist and communist) of the 1930s. The independent and multidisciplinary integration of the social sciences was facilitated by Max Horkheimer, a philosopher, sociologist and social psychologist, who was appointed as director in 1930 and who recruited intellectuals such as Theodor Adorno, a philosopher, sociologist and musicologist, Erich Fromm, a psychoanalyst and Herbert Marcuse, a philosopher. Based on Marx's (1888, p. 423) view that 'philosophers have only interpreted the world … the point is to change it', the critical theory proposed by the Frankfurt School was a social critique intended to effect change. Thus, the methodology of critical theory in this tradition interrogates a subject (a text, a field, a review) with the intention of effecting change (in thinking and practice). This is evident in the present work in our method and in our discussion, especially when we ask questions (a literal form of interrogation) when things (concepts, notions and categories) are ambiguous. The principal method of critical theory in the Frankfurt School was the application of Hegel's dialectical method (and its focus on negation, conflict, contradiction, interrelation and interaction), which Marx drew on to uncover contradictions in predominant ideas of society and social relations. Whilst this present work does not formally use the dialectical method as such, in the discussion section we do analyse contradictions in the field.

Due to the rise of fascism in Germany in the 1930s, the Institute moved from Frankfurt to Geneva and then, in 1935, to New York City. What is referred to as the second phase of the Frankfurt School was marked by two publications – *Dialectic of Enlightenment* (Adorno & Horkheimer, 1947) and *Minima Moralia* (Adorno, 1951) – which shifted the emphasis from a critique of capitalism to a critique of Western civilization; this, in turn, laid the foundation for anti- and post-colonial critiques. As the word suggests, post-colonialism is the critical study of colonialism and imperialism, whereas post-colonial theory refers to a number of theories and theoretical developments that support such critique, such as subjugation (Fanon, 1961), orientalism (Said, 1978), the subaltern (Spivak, 1988) and hybridity (Bhabha, 1994). Post-colonial theory challenges some of the embedded assumptions in the Western intellectual tradition as well as the dominance of the Global North. This is represented in a modest way in this current work, especially in our presentation of the findings in our privileging of the ancient over or before the modern and the Indigenous before the Western.

Deep ecology

Deep ecology describes a diverse and fluid collection of ideas originally based on the paper 'The shallow and the deep, long-range ecology movements', written by the Norwegian philosopher Arne Næss (1973). Although often assumed to be a philosophical position, Næss was adamant that deep ecology is not a philosophy at all but a movement, guided by prevalent

– but not fixed – ideas. One idea common in this movement, which informs the methodology of the present work, is that of ecological self-realization.

In ecological self-realization, human beings are understood to be an ontological part of their wider ecology. Næss (1995) writes:

> What I am suggesting is the supremacy of ecological ontology and a higher realism, over environmental ethics as a means of invigorating the ecology movement in the years to come. If reality is experienced by the ecological Self, our behaviour naturally and beautifully follows norms of strict environmental ethics.
>
> (p. 236)

Note that Næss capitalizes the 'S' to denote a wider and deeper form of selfhood.

Essential to this concept of self is that human beings are part of a higher realism of ecological ontology. That is to say, we are a part of – and subordinate to – the rest of nature as a whole. Also, that the realization of this type of self leads to 'norms of strict environmental ethics', which is to say that motivation to live sustainably and regeneratively can be achieved through the way we experience and conceptualize ecologically what the self is. Finally, Næss asserts that the route to ecological self-realization is through direct experiences of 'free nature' (for example, see Næss, 2005). Because this realization is of a complete, whole, sense of self; it is also intrinsically therapeutic. For example, the etymology of the word healing is the Old English *hælan*, which means 'to make whole'. This establishes a tripartite interrelationship of experiences of nature, the therapeutic process and the practice of living sustainably and regeneratively.

These methodologies have not only informed the method of the research, but have also influenced the presentation of ideas, including the findings of the different approaches to and in the field. Thus, as we are critical of artificial distinctions such as that between 'human' and 'nature', we show this in the findings as we present them. We suggest that this research strategy creates greater philosophical congruence between the subject of enquiry, the method and methodology and the findings, as well as the discussion and conclusion.

2.

Findings

with Ben Classen

In this chapter, we – including our research assistant for the initial project – report our findings.

Initial organization

The initial results were edited and written up in alphabetical order but, very quickly, reorganized into a chronological order – determined either by the first publication within the particular term or by the broader historical view of the discipline or tradition (see Table 2.1). In doing so, we recognized that what may be thought of as Indigenous psychology and psychotherapy date back some centuries, as do shamanic practices, and, similarly, that yoga has been practised in many settings, including outdoors, also for many centuries.

Although this ordering provided some information about the development of the field, especially in the last 40 years, it did not address the fact that these disciplines are different in terms of category. Thus, we considered another way of thinking about categories in terms of the relevant 'ologies' (or study of a subject), 'therapies' and 'practices' (Table 2.2), at which point we deleted reference to 'eco-anxiety', as it is a condition and does not fit within any of these distinctions.

Discipline or tradition	First publication
Indigenous psychology and psychotherapy	–
Shamanic practices	–
Outdoor yoga	–
Rites of passage work	1969
Environmental psychology	1979
Despair and empowerment work	1983
Adventure therapy	1985
Ecopsychology	1992
Ecopsychotherapy	1998
Nature therapy	2004
Terrapsychology	2007
Forest bathing	2007
Wild mindfulness	2010
Nature-based therapy	2011
Wild therapy	2011
Eco-anxiety	2017

Table 2.1. *The chronological order of the findings*

Areas of studies and therapies	Practices
Indigenous psychology Indigenous psychotherapy Environmental psychology Ecopsychology Ecotherapy Ecopsychotherapy Adventure therapy Nature therapy Terrapsychology Nature-based therapy Wild therapy	Shamanistic practice Outdoor yoga Rites of passage work Despair and empowerment work Wild mindfulness Forest bathing

Table 2.2. *The 'ologies', therapies and practices in the field of ecotherapy*

This categorization, however, immediately raised the question of the relationship between psychology and psychotherapy, which is fraught, complex, varied and context dependent. So, finally, we decided on a continuum of ideas and practices in which '...ologies' or fields of study, therapies and specific practices appear in multiple places (Table 2.3). The terms in parentheses in this table are included in order to provide a more complete frame of the field(s) but are not included in the present discussion.

Theory orientation		Practice orientation
Areas of study		
	Therapies	
		Practices
Indigenous psychology Indigenous psychotherapy Environmental psychology Ecopsychology Ecopsychotherapy Terrapsychology	Indigenous psychotherapy (Psychotherapy) Adventure therapy Ecotherapy Ecopsychotherapy Nature therapy Nature-based therapy Wild therapy	Shamanic practice Outdoor yoga (Psychotherapy (modalities) (Counselling) (Clinical psychology) Rites of passage work Despair and empowerment work Forest bathing Wild mindfulness

Table 2.3. *Ecopsychology and ecotherapy practice: a continuum*

Areas of study

Indigenous psychology

Within the literature surveyed, the term 'Indigenous psychology' typically refers to the re-reading of dominant Western approaches to psychology (Kim & Berry, 1993). Generally, research in this area is focused on reconfiguring psychological theory and practice in a way that is more relevant to the cultural contexts and worldviews of non-Western populations. As Kim and Berry (1993, p. 2) put it, Indigenous psychology is 'the scientific study of human behaviour or mind that is native, that is not transported from other regions, and that is designed for its people'.

Academics publishing in this area generally advocate for a reconstitution or indigenizing (Danziger, 2006) of psychological praxis that better acknowledges and/or accommodates Indigenous perspectives (Kim *et al.*, 2016). Much research, however, is complicated by a number of theoretical issues, including the usual disagreements and uncertainties about definitions, as well as a certain competition with other similar and more established fields of cultural and cross-cultural psychology: all of which, Jahoda (2016) suggests, has resulted in a dwindling of research outputs and impact in this field.

Ideologically, Indigenous psychology is aligned with many of the other fields covered in this review. The value of, and need for, psychological perspectives that consider the values, belief systems and cultural contexts of Indigenous populations has been discussed by many authors (e.g. Ho, 1998; Yang, 2000). Given the traditionally close connections between Indigenous populations and their ecology, it seems likely that an Indigenous – or indigenized – psychology would be one that places some emphasis on ecological concerns. However, somewhat surprisingly, the Indigenous psychology literature does not offer a substantial consideration of ecological perspectives. This may be because those writing about Indigenous psychology have, strategically, been focused more on the theory, practice and institutions of Western psychology, than on those of the Indigenous world. This is, however, changing, for instance, in research with demands for data sovereignty (Global Indigenous Data Alliance, 2019; Taylor & Kukutai, 2016), and, in education, with initiatives designed to decolonize the curriculum (Morreira *et al.*, 2021).

In the ecopsychology literature, Jones and Segal (2018) provide a detailed discussion of the value of ecopsychological perspectives that are mindful of – and seek to address – traditional colonialist perspectives on psychological wellbeing. Fisher (2019) argues that the conceptual disconnect between people and their ecology, which ecopsychology seeks to repair, is largely thanks to the cultural separation of people from the natural environment brought about by Western, industrial society. Based on this, he put forward ecopsychology as a form of decolonial praxis. Although Fisher does not use the term 'Indigenous psychology', the focus of his article is on the role of natural environments in the psychological experience of Indigenous populations. Drawing more precise links between Indigenous psychology and the ecopsychological literature may be a useful addition to further research.

Indigenous psychotherapy

Indigenous psychotherapy, or Indigenous psychological therapy, encompasses a broad field of literature which aligns with most of the other ideas covered in this review. Like the relationship between ecotherapy and ecopsychology, Indigenous therapy might best be understood as efforts to apply Indigenous psychological perspectives in professional therapeutic practice. However, this distinction is not evident within the literature, with terms such as 'Indigenous psychology', 'Indigenous psychiatry' and 'Indigenous psychotherapy' used interchangeably. Much of the literature in this field is focused on attempts to integrate Indigenous culture, beliefs and practices into traditional Western psychotherapy (Allison *et al.*, 1994; Bernal & Castro, 1994; Sue, 2003; Sue & Zane, 1987), and ranges from general cultural competence among therapists (Sue *et al.*, 2009), through to Western therapists adopting traditional Indigenous approaches to healing into their practice (Gone, 2010). Mohatt (2010, p. 237) refers to the latter practice as 'seeking to find the human without separating the person from his or her culture'.

In a recent review of Indigenous mental health research, Gone and Kirmayer (2020) contend that indigeneity and colonization histories are deeply entangled – both directly and indirectly. Together and separately (e.g. Gone, 2008; Kirmayer, 2007), they offer three understandings of indigeneity which might be used to guide practice that is sensitive to the needs of Indigenous populations:

> as a social-historical understanding of communities as First Peoples, which necessarily includes the long shadow cast by colonization even as this is now lived and expressed in relation to political agency. A second meaning of indigeneity entails land-based notions of personhood

> as connected to particular places grounded in local ecologies, through cultural knowledge and practices … A third meaning of indigeneity entails notions of cosmology, ceremony and the sacred, which relate Indigenous communities to potent spiritual persons and powers, and express culturally specific values of divinity, community, morality, and well-being (i.e. living a good life).
>
> (Gone & Kirmayer, 2020, p. 238)

Despite centring relationships between human beings and the rest of nature in approaches to Indigenous therapy, Gone and Kirmayer (2020) fall short of specifically recommending how a therapist might draw on the environment in Indigenous mental health practice. Indeed, much of the literature on Indigenous psychotherapy recognizes the importance of the natural environment or, we prefer, ecology, yet it is only briefly discussed as one aspect of broader cultural competence and awareness within Indigenous mental health care (Mikahere-Hall *et al.*, 2019). Moylan (2009) explores using Indigenous approaches to psychotherapy that reflect the environment, when working with Australian Aboriginal people living with depression. Specific recommendations for practice include:

> Look at how Indigenous people would like to be healed. Gradually look at the lifestyle of Indigenous people and what makes them relax, for example, family, fishing, and gardening … Always try to sit on the ground, cross-legged. Sitting on the mat, floor, ground, is more calming … Photographs from local features of the land are very

> helpful as a starting point for therapy. It is a way of bringing country and spirit into therapy.
>
> (pp. 183–184)

Similarly, Mwiti (2014, p. 176) notes the importance of including care for the environment in practice with Indigenous African populations arguing that 'psychotherapists in Africa cannot divorce their care for people from their care for creation and the environment. Healthy farms, full crops, clean water, healthy bodies, clean homes, fresh air, and a balanced diet are all part of psychotherapy and wholeness'.

Earlier, Lee (2002) expounded on the concept of 'wholeness' in their review of Indigenous Chinese approaches to health care, contending that living in harmony with nature is an essential character of psychotherapy as informed by Chinese philosophy, specifically a Taoist worldview. In Chinese Indigenous (psycho) therapies, to achieve bio-psycho-emotional–socio-spiritual balance, a person is expected to live in harmony with the universe and other people. Based on the moral and social principles of Confucianism, people are treated and helped without being separated from their families, communities and cultural groups. In this way, Chinese people are viewed as more receptive to a holistic approach for dealing with their emotional and life issues (Lee, 2002).

In summary, in Indigenous psychotherapy the role of the environment seems to be widely recognized as important. However, substantive recommendations regarding how an Indigenous psychological or psychotherapeutic conception of nature might be drawn upon in therapeutic practice seem sporadic. As with Indigenous psychology, Western psychotherapy research into indigeneity primarily focuses on incorporating Indigenous cultural beliefs into Western therapeutic approaches and not the other way around – or, perhaps more radically, in looking to a genuine bicultural encounter (for an example of which, see Rivers *et al.*, 2022).

Environmental psychology

Closely related but conceptually distinct from ecopsychology is the study of the psychological impacts of any environment on the human organism. This can include natural, wild, built, managed, and technologically mediated and virtual environments. This study tends to privilege analysis over praxis and is usually less political than ecopsychology. For example, ecopsychology often calls for some form of activism to achieve ecological sustainability, whereas environmental psychology may provide analysis without any commentary on what should or should not be done. In this sense, environmental psychology fits the traditional ideas of conventional empirical science more directly than ecopsychology, aspiring to be somewhat value neutral. This is in sharp contrast to the implicit counter-culturalism of ecopsychology, which demands a fundamental shift in our conceptions of self, nature, and reality.

Despite their differences, the terms ecopsychology and environmental psychology are used interchangeably within the literature. Debates about their philosophy and terminology, particularly with environmental psychology, are formidably dense (Panov, 2017). In some cases, environmental psychology is used to refer to an approach to psychology centred on the abstract notion of an individual's personal psychosocial 'ecology', for example, their relationship with and perception of a range of subjective ideas, experiences, people and places (von Eckartsberg, 1979). Although relevant in terms of some aspects of an individual's relationships with the natural environment, there is a theoretical distinction to be made between this and their psychological relationship with the physical ecology of the natural world, which might be less subjective, for example, sensory experiences of natural ecosystems that affect the individual beyond their control.

The literature suggests that a primary focus of contemporary environmental psychology is the impact of climate change on mental wellbeing, which argues that climate change is causing more extreme and unpredictable weather events and that these affect mental wellbeing. For example, Hayes *et al.* (2018) outline three ways in which climate change impacts mental health outcomes. First, direct consequences where trauma is related to extreme weather events like floods, cyclones, heat waves and wildfires. Second, indirect consequences including trauma related to social, economic and environmental disruptions, including famine, civil conflict, displacement and migration. Third, overarching consequences such as long-term emotional distress due to increased awareness of the threats and impacts of climate change. It is the last of these ecologically induced mental health issues that falls closest to the ecopsychology and ecotherapy literature. Note that, although we prefer the term 'global warming' to 'climate change', we recognize that the two are used synonymously.

Although ample literature exists examining the impact of adverse weather events on mental health, studies typically treat these as isolated and unconnected incidents, and often fail to make explicit the 'climate change–weather events–mental health' link. This fosters what Hayes *et al.* (2018, p. 3) refer to as 'a reactive culture of emergency response'. Furthermore, much of the literature focuses on the direct effects of climate change-induced weather events on mental health during and after the event, with little consideration for the pre-event psychology of individuals who are acutely aware of the oncoming and ongoing consequences of climate change, for example, heightened anxiety, sense of loss, feelings of impending doom, helplessness and fatalism – which has been termed 'eco-anxiety' or 'ecological grief' (Usher *et al.*, 2019).

Climate change and its mental health consequences tend to affect marginalized populations, including Indigenous and ethnic minority populations, disproportionately (Intergovernmental Panel on Climate Change, 2018). Further research exploring the links of eco-anxiety, Indigenous therapy practice and traditional relationships between Indigenous populations and the land is of growing importance in the environmental psychology field, blurring its boundaries with ecopsychology further.

Ecopsychology

Ecopsychology explores all aspects of human psychology as it relates to the rest of nature (by which we mean nature including human beings). Where other psychological approaches focus on the alienation between one person and another, a person and their family or a person and society, ecopsychology focuses on the more fundamental alienation between the psyche of industrial growth culture and its physical environment (Roszak, 1992). This includes, for example: the psychological impacts of ecological issues on the way people think, feel and behave; psychological phenomena arising from people being in a range of natural environments; the social and cultural psychology of ecologically unsustainable behaviours; and the treatment of mental health issues through outdoor experiences.

Theodore Roszak's (1992) book *The Voice of the Earth* and his collaborative, edited volume, *Ecopsychology: Restoring the Earth, Healing the Mind* (Roszak *et al.*, 1995) are widely credited with popularizing the term ecopsychology. In these works, a core tenet is that an individual's environment, and the quality of their engagement with that environment, is directly related to their psychological wellbeing. According to Fisher (2016, p. 3), 'Roszak wanted ecopsychology to be a force for a more psychologically literate environmentalism, replacing strategies based on guilt and fear with ones that draw on people's inherent love and compassion for the earth.' Roszak's edited volume (1995) also established ecopsychology as a radically plural discipline. Intersections of ecopsychology, ethnicity and indigeneity (Armstrong, 1995), race (Anthony, 1995) and gender (Gomes & Kanner, 1995), together with critiques of industrial growth culture (Glendinning, 1995) and consumerism (Kanner & Gomes, 1995), all first found a voice within this seminal text. This diversity, alongside clear calls for personal and social action, linked psychology directly with ecology and, crucially, with activism. It is this triangulation that differentiates ecopsychology most clearly from other forms.

Since its early development, for example, by Shepard (1982), Roszak (1992) and Abram (1996), several critiques have been levelled at the methodological legitimacy of ecopsychology, especially from an empirical perspective. Reser (1995) and Clayton and Myers (2009) have offered critiques of ecopsychology as a specific field, claiming that it is poorly defined and could simply be one that is already adequately covered by other established psychological categories, such as environmental, social and transpersonal psychology. Furthermore, these authors contend that: ecopsychology has misappropriated Indigenous perspectives and practices; conflated ecological immorality with mental illness – for example, that mistreatment of, or disregard for, the environment is grounds for insanity, as distinct from simply being an example of irrational, short-sighted or ignorant behaviour; and that 'primacy [is] given to direct experience at the expense of a more objective account of the nature of such experiences' (Reser, 1995, p. 246).

These critiques have resulted in significant tension within the field and have led to a schism between what Fisher (2013a) refers to as first-generation and second-generation ecopsychology. This second-generation of ecopsychology can be dated from the founding of the peer-review journal

Ecopsychology in 2009. In its inaugural issue, Doherty (2009) called for the need for approaches to ecopsychology theory and practice to be more pragmatic and empirically minded than had historically been the case. He proposed that this would benefit the field by improving its integration and acceptance within more traditional psychological theory, a perspective also supported by Kahn and Hasbach (2012). Others, however, have pushed back against what they perceive to be a tempering of the origins and radical contribution of ecopsychology. For example, Fisher (2013b) argues that ecopsychology is fundamentally radical and that to bring ecopsychology theory and practice into line with more mainstream theoretical standards and frameworks is to undermine its true, counter-cultural, nature.

Ecopsychotherapy

Burns (1998, p. 19) argues for the use of the term ecopsychotherapy as distinct from ecotherapy, claiming that, 'As a term, ecotherapy does not fully do justice to the concept that it seeks to communicate … [and] is misleading, because it is not the ecology that is the subject of treatment'. Instead, Burns delineates ecopsychotherapy as including 'the concepts of both the human mind and the environment. It assumes that there is a dynamic process taking place between the two, not only for healing but also for an ongoing state of well-being' (p. 20). Yet, despite differentiating between the terms, Burns goes on to use the word ecotherapy in his book, because the 'nomenclature is less cumbersome, and …

because it is more akin to the terminology of other writers and workers in this field. In general, the words nature-guided therapy, ecopsychotherapy, and ecotherapy will be seen as synonymous' (p. 21).

The synonymous use of ecopsychotherapy, ecotherapy and nature-guided or -based therapy is reflected in the literature where searches for 'ecopsychotherapy' are just as likely to turn up articles and book chapters that primarily refer to 'ecotherapy'. If anything, 'ecopsychotherapy' is used far less frequently than other similar terms. One potentially useful distinction, however, is that ecopsychotherapy more often refers to therapist-centred outdoor practice. For example, where a psychotherapist practises within their registered modality but works with their client outside instead of indoors. In this case, the modality, which is centred in the therapist, takes precedence over the location. This is evidenced by conventionally qualified and registered psychotherapists who explicitly refer to themselves as ecopsychotherapists (Haughey, 2016).

Rust (2020) adds more clarity:

> Ecopsychotherapy is a relatively new form of psychotherapy which understands that human relationships exist within the larger context of our life on earth … Psychotherapy invites us to tell the story of our human relationships; ecopsychotherapy expands this to include our earth story, the context in which our human relationships sit.
>
> (p. 1)

This definition, however, could simply extend established notions of psychotherapy into the ecological realm, while maintaining a therapist- and modality-centred approach. This would maintain current and mainstream forms, contrary to the call for ecopsychology and its many modes of application, arguably including ecopsychotherapy, to remain firmly radical. Interestingly, Rust adds, 'Ecopsychotherapy is just one of many ecotherapies which arise out of the field of ecopsychology, [and] the inquiry into our human relationship with the rest of nature' (Rust, 2020, p. 1). This places ecopsychotherapy in a hierarchy of broader and more generic contexts, while aligning it specifically to psychotherapy as a professional community. This both fits with the wider literature and suggests yet another dark grey area in defining the field of ecotherapy as a whole.

Terrapsychology

Terrapsychology is the study of how terrain, place, element and natural processes show up in human psychology, endeavour and story, including myths and legends. It is based on the premise that we are not separate from the sites in which we live and work. In this perspective, understanding *what* we do and *who* we are requires understanding of *where* we are.

The term terrapsychology is most strongly associated with the work of Chalquist (2011, 2020), an American academic and therapist who has written several books on the subject. He defines terrapsychology as a transdisciplinary study of the presence of the outer world within the human psyche.

The term terrapsychology is rarely used outside Chalquist's own publications, or publications with which he has been associated (e.g. Häber, 2020). Terrapsychology is only marginally distinguishable from what elsewhere is referred to as ecopsychology, the main distinction being a more explicit emphasis on Jungian archetypes, mythical storytelling and folklore (see Chalquist, 2020). In this sense, terrapsychology can be understood as a psychology of re-enchantment of our relations with the world, and therefore with each other (Chalquist, 2007).

Therapies

Adventure therapy

Adventure therapy is grounded in the traditions of experiential learning (Dewey, 1938), which is a broad field of research and practice fundamentally centred around direct, multisensory physical experiences as a means of learning (Kraft & Sakofs, 1985). An important feature of this approach is allowing individuals the time and space for planning, theorizing and reflection around performing specific physical activities. It is the therapeutic application of this 'experiential learning cycle' (Kolb, 2014) that is the emphasis of adventure therapy (Crisp, 1998). Adapting Kraft and Sakofs' (1985) earlier work, Gass (1993) characterizes adventure therapy as follows:

- The client becomes a participant rather than a spectator in therapy.

- Therapeutic activities require client motivation in the form of energy, involvement and responsibility.
- Therapeutic activities are real and meaningful in terms of natural consequences for the client.
- Reflection is a critical element of the therapeutic process.
- Functional change must have present as well as future relevance for clients and their society.

It is important to note the absence of nature in this characterization, beyond its indirect potential to provide the 'natural consequences' identified as offering meaning to the client.

Priest (2021, pp. 2–3) argues that 'nature not only causes the natural consequences for learning in adventure, it also provides recuperative qualities'. However, these recuperative qualities are framed as secondary to the primary benefits of adventure itself. Priest (2021, p. 2) writes, 'By applying competence against the risks, clients are able to resolve the uncertainty of the adventure in a favourable manner. Repeated successes, carefully facilitated by staff, result in improved resilience, confidence, and self-esteem'.

The focus is on adventure as the therapeutic mode and nature is left as a setting that can provide uncertainty and some additional, yet unexplained, recuperative benefits. In fact, much adventure therapy practice was developed through the 'Adventure-Based Learning' (ABL) movement using human-built 'high ropes' courses. Although these structures are often outdoors, they do not need to be, and the outdoor setting is not integral to the process. In many cases, indoor settings are used to good effect (Rohnke, 1986).

Ultimately, there is a general assumption that adventure therapy takes place outdoors. However, there is no significant analysis of the role of nature itself, beyond its generic potential to provide the sense of risk and uncertainty at the heart of this approach.

Confusion exists within the adventure therapy community because the word 'adventure' is usually associated with activities that take place outdoors (for example, hiking, rock climbing, kayaking, mountaineering, rafting, etc.). This implies that adventure therapy is the same as other outdoor approaches. The term is therefore often incorrectly interchanged with wilderness therapy, wild therapy, ecotherapy and other specifically outdoor-based approaches.

Newes and Bandoroff (2004) also note that Gass' principles are not unique to adventure therapy and can be seen as essential elements of general therapeutic practice. They argue that 'therapists are able to use any type of therapeutic orientation they adhere to in the processing that occurs' (Newes & Bandoroff, 2004, p. 4). However, what separates adventure therapy, as an approach from therapy *per se*, is the medium through which the therapeutic process is realized: active, somatic physical experiences with potentially uncertain outcomes. Thus, at the heart of adventure therapy lies a client having a somatic experience of their physical surroundings involving a sense of uncertainty and risk – alongside an opportunity to process that experience in a structured and supported way.

There is contention surrounding the naming of adventure therapy and the qualification of its practitioners. As well as often being assumed to take place outdoors, 'adventure' equally does not necessarily refer to adrenaline-seeking, action-packed experiences. Less physically demanding experiences can be utilized – there just needs to be a sense of uncertainty, which can be experienced along a very broad continuum. This means that practitioners do not necessarily need to be professionally qualified or experienced outdoor leaders. In a similar way, controversy exists within the field surrounding adventure programmes that are geared towards therapeutic outcomes that are not delivered solely by professionals with formal therapeutic qualifications – although a lack of formal credentials does not necessarily mean that an individual is unequipped to facilitate therapeutic outcomes in certain contexts. This controversy extends into a debate about the extent to which adventure therapy should be held to the same clinical standards as other approaches to therapy (Newes & Bandoroff, 2004).

Although some approaches to adventure therapy incorporate one-to-one work, typically it involves groups of between six and fourteen at-risk youths or adolescents (Bacon & Kimball, 1989; Caulkins *et al.*, 2006; Hill, 2007). It originated and is most commonly found in traditional youth outdoor learning contexts.

Ecotherapy

The term ecotherapy was first coined by Howard Clinebell (1996) and is an approach to therapy that aims to bring individuals into a deeper relationship with their natural environment (Wolsko & Hoyt, 2012). Although Buzzell and Chalquist (2009) use the term ecotherapy to develop an approach to therapeutic practice that draws upon both ecopsychology and psychotherapy, attempts have been made to reclaim the term ecotherapy as one that explicitly refers to a form of ecologically focused therapy (Hasbach, 2012). That said, ecotherapy is considered to be an umbrella term that accommodates all current approaches to the practical application of ecopsychology (Rust, 2020). Ecotherapy can take the form of a range of applications (Roszak *et al.*, 1995), many of which overlap, and can be applied to a diversity of existing approaches to psychosocial practice, for example, in social work (Norton, 2009). Although the outputs and experiences of ecotherapy are often difficult to quantify, there is a considerable amount of contemporary research that is finding ways of doing this (for instance, Ibes *et al.*, 2018).

Ecotherapy is supported by a range of literature about the evolutionary psychological predisposition humans have towards natural environments – as opposed to industrial and urban environments (Kellert & Wilson, 1993; Orians, 1986). Through somatic experiences of natural environments, ecotherapy gives a client the opportunity to recontextualize their personal experiences within a broader, environmental context (Kaplan & Talbot, 1983). Outside, and before, the influence of the ecopsychology movement, ecotherapy has a long history within psychological treatment, for example, the use of gardens and 'green spaces' by nineteenth-century institutions (Wilson *et al.*, 2008). This tradition declined throughout the twentieth century as the development of evidence-based practice privileged quantitative studies of treatment efficacy with clearly defined parameters and variables. This disadvantaged ecotherapy where the most helpful data are often qualitative (Coote *et al.*, 2004). More recently, in the twenty-first century, ecotherapy has seen a resurgence, with practices including gardening, walking groups and conservation work being reported as successfully improving people's mental health (MIND, 2007). The publication of the MIND report, in particular, has led to the term ecotherapy being widely used throughout the United Kingdom (and beyond) to refer to any sort of outdoor activity done with the intention of improving mental health (Jordan, 2016).

Despite the interest in ecotherapy, methodological limitations pose a consistent challenge to evaluating its efficacy empirically. Although Wilson *et al.* (2008) primarily focus on exposure to, and immersion in, green spaces as a form of ecotherapy, they note four key methodological challenges that are broadly applicable across a range of ecotherapy practices:

1. Establishing control groups and controlling variables in a natural environment;
2. Direction of relationships and causality;
3. Reliance on self-report measures; and
4. Non-validated questionnaires.

Although meeting these challenges is by no means essential to all forms of credible research, doing so does help make findings comparable to other practices and approaches. Given that many of these other comparable practices also tend to subscribe to more conventional ideas about empiricism, for example, those that are cognitive and behavioural, they tend to gain greater mainstream credibility and resources, privileging them over ecotherapy.

Nature therapy

Within the literature, the term nature therapy is synonymous with ecotherapy. Thus, Berger (2008) uses the term to refer to what elsewhere is considered as ecotherapy or ecopsychotherapy. His work centres on the development of practice frameworks (Berger, 2008; Berger & Tiry, 2012), where the natural environment is seen as a living, dynamic partner in the therapeutic process, rather than simply a background or setting where therapy can take place (Berger, 2004).

Beyond Berger, most other search results for nature therapy appear to be related to the Japanese practice of shinrin-yoku, or forest bathing (see below). However, although forest bathing is primarily a sort of therapy via osmosis, Berger's nature therapy is more directly focused on a skilled practitioner facilitating a therapeutic process outdoors. Nature therapy, then, is another good example of a generic term for outdoor therapies.

Nature-based therapy

The literature on nature-based therapy draws attention to the historical use of gardens and greenspaces in mental health institutions, as well as general hospitals and other medical institutions (Gullone, 2000; Stigsdotter *et al.*, 2011).

Interestingly, some of the most prolific authors who use the term are from Scandinavia and western Europe, which suggests that the overlap between terms such as nature therapy, ecotherapy and outdoor therapy might be explained to a certain extent by geographical preferences and ambiguous translations. However, searches for nature therapy that included the term nature-*based* therapy throw up a mix of outdoor activities aimed at achieving therapeutic outcomes. As Sahlin *et al.* (2012) observe:

> Nature-Based Therapeutic (NBT) programs have increased in number in Sweden during the past decade. These programs often comprise two parts: (1) traditional medical rehabilitation methods used for stress-related disorders which are professionally integrated into a nature context; and (2) activities, or simply being, in a garden and/or nature.
>
> (p. 9)

The term nature-based therapy is used here to refer to what we have come to understand from the literature as both ecotherapy and ecopsychotherapy. It is also used to describe a combination of the two.

Nature-based therapy, therefore, seems to be another catch-all term. For example, Oh *et al.* (2020) used nature-based therapy as synonymous with forest bathing, whereas Segal *et al.* (2020) discussed nature-based therapy in terms of a traditional client–therapist relationship being transposed from an indoor context to an outdoor one. Stigsdotter *et al.* (2011)

also group together ecotherapy, ecological psychotherapy, conservation therapy, nature-assisted therapy, nature-guided therapy and nature therapy, recognizing that, although these terms appear to refer to distinct approaches, they all derive from the notion that people and the rest of nature can heal each other in various ways.

Stigsdotter *et al.* (2011) recognize the overlap and confusion in terminology. They sought to distinguish between nature-based therapy via osmosis and nature-based therapy guided by a therapist contending that they are:

> two different phenomena. One concern designing and/or planning nature settings or gardens for the improvement or maintenance of people's health. This could be for a certain group of patients or for the general public. We define this as 'health design and planning'. On the other hand, we are dealing with the phenomenon of using a certain setting, specially designed or specially chosen, for a therapeutic intervention. We define this as a 'nature-based therapeutic intervention'.
>
> (p. 313)

Included in their definition of nature-based therapeutic interventions are activities such as horticultural therapy, social and therapeutic horticulture, and care farms, which further exacerbate the challenges of overlapping terminology. These and other similar terms refer to using gardening activities and projects as a form of therapeutic intervention, a practice that originally grew out of occupational therapy

(Relf & Dorn, 1995). The use of horticultural therapy for the treatment of British and US soldiers after the First and Second World Wars saw this form of therapy become closely aligned with the treatment of post-traumatic stress disorder (Shoemaker, 2002). Since the 1950s and 1960s, horticultural therapy has been developed for use in the treatment of a wide range of mental health and physiological challenges, including strokes, cardiovascular issues and anxiety (Söderback *et al.*, 2004). 'Care farms', 'green care' and other related terms refer to nature-based therapeutic interventions in a farm context which, typically, incorporate some form of animal-assisted therapy (Hassink & Van Dijk, 2006).

Wild therapy

Wild therapy was first proposed by Totton (2011) in his book *Wild Therapy: Undomesticating our Inner and Outer Worlds.* Totton argued that traditional approaches to therapy are poorly equipped to adapt to ecopsychological perspectives, and often suffer from an over-emphasis on rationality and order. Totton presented wild therapy as a means for re-envisioning therapeutic practice as a 'less tame' approach to traditional forms of therapy (Totton, 2013). In doing so, Totton explicitly draws on an ecopsychological conception of the self, which places human beings as fundamentally embedded within nature, thereby framing wild therapy as an ecosystemic model (Potgieter, 2018). Totton argues that human beings have become 'domesticated', that is, alienated from raw emotional experiences and impulses, and that wild therapy is a means of 'un-domesticating' ourselves and our experiences (Priestman, 2015).

Unlike some of the more generic literature on ecotherapy, Totton (2013) provides clear details of what is actually involved in the practice of wild therapy:

> At the most concrete level, the practice consists of moving into the outdoors from a 'base camp', which might be the therapy room or a literal camp in a relatively wild area; spending some time there, and then returning and integrating what has happened. The journey can be accompanied or unaccompanied; the time may be spent moving around or finding and staying in one spot; the process may take half an hour, or a whole day. There are many possible variations on this straightforward structure.
>
> (p. 1)

Interestingly, the clear focus on three stages of the therapeutic process – moving into the outdoors from a base camp (separation), spending time in the outdoors (liminality) and returning and integrating what was experienced outdoors of pre-separation and liminal experiences (incorporation) – are consistent with the breakdown of a rite of passage process as identified by Turner *et al.* (1969). As this pattern is extremely common in the structure of many kinds of outdoor programmes, whether framed as therapeutic or not, the central practical tenets of wild therapy appear to be consistent with numerous other generic forms of outdoor practice.

Practices

Shamanic practice

According to Berger and McLeod (2006, p. 80), 'The concept of conducting transformative and healing work in nature is not new; it can be traced back to ancient times when people lived in communities in nature.' Shamanism describes a diverse range of culturally embedded, ancient sacred practices. A shaman is typically defined as an individual who enters a trance-like state and provides guidance and healing to other members of the community, including, but not limited to, matters regarding physiological and mental health and wellbeing (Walsh, 1989). Shamanism is believed to have been largely ubiquitous throughout history among Indigenous and tribal societies (Singh, 2018).

Shamanic ceremonies are often highly ritualized and intimate, aiming to bring about psychological and/or physiological ease, a characteristic shared by many Western therapeutic approaches (Al-Krenawi, 1999). Like Indigenous psychotherapy, shamanic practice often draws on the relationships between human beings and their natural environment as a means of addressing health challenges. As such, shamans might, in some ways, be regarded as the original ecotherapists. As Berger and McLeod (2006, p. 80) put it: shamans 'incorporate nature's health powers … to help people recover from illness, cope with the unknown, and make the transition from one status to another'. However, transposing shamanic practices into a contemporary Western therapeutic context as ecotherapy presents some significant appropriation issues. These are discussed later, along with other practices that show similar tendencies.

Outdoor yoga

Yoga is an ancient spiritual practice originating in India. It has been widely adopted in the West where practitioners have tended to focus on its physical and mental health benefits – in some cases to the detriment of its more spiritual aspects (Singleton, 2010). Most contemporary Western yoga practice involves a focus on holding physical postures, transitioning between postures in flowing sequences, sometimes including a focus on breathing exercises and often involving a period of relaxation towards the end of the session (Newcombe, 2009). The slow, controlled and often self-reflective nature of yoga lends itself to somatic therapeutic practice and often leads to a range of psychological benefits (Khalsa, 2013; Nagendra, 2013).

To date, outdoor yoga has not appeared much in ecotherapy-related literature. Where it does, it might be best understood as an example of 'green exercise' (Buckley, 2020; Kulas, 2019; Lehto *et al.*, 2006). Instead of considering outdoor yoga as a therapeutic approach distinct from general yoga, the outdoors is often treated simply as an alternative setting (Elwy *et al.*, 2014). For example, Kim *et al.* (2016, p. 441) consider the benefits of yoga for the physical and psychological health of school-aged children; they write: 'On the last field trip, the children visited a local park where they joined in an outdoor yoga program. Afterward, they talked about how nature helped relax their body and mind.' Zak (2020) also considers outdoor 'nature yoga' in relation to children, noting that:

> Nature yoga in outdoor, informal education programs then is sure to have a positive impact on the physical, emotional, and mental health of children … Ideally, it is practised outside in a natural area, but this is not a requirement. Additional mindfulness practices complement yoga sessions of age-appropriate length encourage storytelling, wandering, mapping, gratitude, using all the senses, and mimicking animal forms, behaviours, and vocalizations out in nature.
>
> (pp. 1–2)

Without any research clearly demonstrating the benefits of outdoor yoga over any other form of yoga, or of its development as a distinctly ecopsychological approach to therapy, it may best be understood as an established traditional practice sometimes informally relocated into an outdoor setting.

Despair and empowerment work

Macy is a renowned scholar whose work is widely cited in discussions about the psychological impacts of social and environmental uncertainty. As her earlier work, *Despair and Personal Power in the Nuclear Age* (Macy, 1983) attests, her approach was originally developed in response to the nuclear threats of the 1980s. However, as the Cold War ended, and concurrent with increasing awareness of catastrophic environmental issues, the focus of her work shifted.

Today Macy's work deals with the existential despair associated with global ecological crises, which, in turn, is directly related to eco-anxiety (Buzzell & Chalquist, 2009). Building on Macy's work, R. Lertzman (2015), a psychotherapist and researcher, considers treatment approaches to what she calls 'environmental melancholia', much of which is focused on dealing with feelings of loss and mourning related to environmental degradation.

Conn (1990) is another therapist and teacher whose work focuses on the psychology of global awareness and social responsibility and is directly informed by Macy's (1983) despair and empowerment work. Conn (1992) outlines a definition and motive for her practice:

> The basic challenge of an ecologically responsible psychotherapy, or ecotherapy, is to look at therapy as a place where the personal problems brought by clients, the so-called personal stories, can be seen not only in their vivid particularities but also as microcosms of the larger whole, of what is happening in the larger world … As we develop a way of connecting the self and the world, then the goals of therapy become not just personal release but also participation in and contribution to the healing of the world.
>
> (pp. 3–4)

Between them, Macy (1983), Conn (1990) and R. Lertzman (2015) draw attention to the process of a client 'connecting' with the source of environmental grief and despair. This provides a means of addressing symptoms that are a consequence of environmental trauma. Equally important to the treatment of symptoms in Macy's work is that engaging directly with ecological trauma, in a structured and supported way, can provide catharsis, challenge denial, encourage creativity and increase a sense of belonging to a group with shared concerns. This can empower people to take action to address ecological challenges, forming the 'empowerment' aspect of the work.

Macy's work, which is well established, has the potential to provide a clearly discernible framework for developing ecotherapy practices that might address experiences of eco-anxiety, climate grief and ecological trauma. However, Macy's work does not, either by definition or usually in practice, take place outdoors. This differentiates it clearly from other forms of ecologically focused work that do.

Rites of passage work

Rites of passage are typically heavily ritualized processes through which an individual marks a significant symbolic transition from one stage of life into the next (Turner, 1987; Turner *et al.*, 1969; Van Gennep, 2019). These rituals are most frequently associated with Indigenous communities, which have continuous traditions from ancient times, for example, the 'vision quest' of some American First Peoples and the 'walkabout' of some Australian Aboriginal cultures. Historically, they were also an important part of Western traditions, but they are rarely referred to as rites of passage today. However, they can be readily observed in present-day practices such as pilgrimage, marriage, baptism, and many other religious and secular events.

Although a rite of passage ceremony is traditionally associated with reformation of a person's social standing, this process often necessitates a renegotiation of their sense of self (Schouten, 1991). The book *The Ritual Process: Structure and Anti-Structure* (Turner *et al.*, 1969) is one of the most widely cited ethnographic studies of rites of passage. Here the authors define a rite of passage as involving three essential stages: (1) separation, wherein the individual withdraws or detaches from their previous psychosocial state and prepares to enter a new one; (2) liminality, an ambiguous space of transition, wherein the individual finds themselves in between their old and new selves; and (3) incorporation, wherein the individual aggregates their new experiences with their past, returning to the world with a renewed sense of self and identity. These phases can, to a greater or lesser extent, be broadly mapped onto a range of approaches to therapeutic practice, and the therapist and location of the therapy can be seen to be a facilitator of the rite of passage (Beels, 2007).

Many outdoor personal development and wilderness therapy programmes are explicitly informed by rites of passage work (Russell, 2001, 2006; Ungar *et al.*, 2005). In some cases, these programmes involve emphasizing the connection between the natural environment and the psyche of the individual (Schell-Faucon, 2001). Others explicitly draw upon Indigenous cultural knowledge, values and practices surrounding human connection with the land, and incorporate these into the process (D. A. Lertzman, 2002). Parallels are often drawn between the three essential stages of a rite of passage ritual and the process of undertaking a 'solo', where the individual journeys away from other people, daily life and familiar surroundings into an outdoor, often confronting, wild natural environment. The process ends with the individual returning to their daily life with a reconstituted understanding of themselves and their world (Andrews, 1999).

Norris (2011, p. 117) critiques the use of rites of passage work to inform outdoor therapy citing cultural misappropriation: 'The use of Indigenous ritual and symbolic motifs by non-Indigenous educators can be an act of cultural misappropriation and an extension of colonialism.' Oles (1995) suggests that such practices lose their meaning and authenticity outside the cultural and community contexts from which they emerged. This is a critical issue for many Indigenous people and some groups and nations have made formal declarations decrying the appropriation of their cultural traditions and practices. Smith (1999, p. 159) reflects that the protection of such traditions and knowledge is 'a deep need linked to the survival of Indigenous peoples'. On this basis, it is clearly unacceptable for the Western cultures that forced this need for survival through genocide and colonization to then appropriate practices for their own benefit. As previously noted, cultural misappropriation of practices is discussed later.

Forest bathing

Forest bathing, also known as 'shinrin-yoku', is a form of ecotherapy that involves spending time immersed in a forest environment (Song *et al.*, 2016). The practice has existed as a means of improving and maintaining mental health within Japanese culture since the early 1980s and is consistently associated with improved physical and mental health outcomes (Hansen *et al.*, 2017).

Forest bathing, and its synonym forest therapy, is a state-endorsed activity in Japan and South Korea. In South Korea, it is defined by law as a set of 'immune-strengthening and health-promoting activities utilizing various elements of the forest such as fragrance and scenic view' (Jung *et al.*, 2015, p. 274). The Japanese Forestry Agency even certify specific forests in which to conduct therapy (Rajoo *et al.*, 2020).

A sizeable body of Japanese-based research demonstrates the health benefits of forest bathing (Ideno *et al.*, 2017; Kamioka *et al.*, 2012; Kotera *et al.*, 2020; Li, 2018; Morita *et al.*, 2007; Tsunetsugu *et al.*, 2010). A systematic review conducted by Rajoo *et al.* (2020) provides a comprehensive view of forest bathing outcomes and practices.

Most studies of the psychosocial outcomes of forest bathing use self-report questionnaires to assess the overall mental health and emotional states of participants, for example, the Profile of Mood States and the Total Mood Disturbance tool (Furuyashiki *et al.*, 2019), the Positive and Negative Affect Schedule (Markwell & Gladwin, 2020) and the Depression Anxiety Stress Scale (Rajoo *et al.*, 2020). Rajoo *et al.* note several methodological concerns, including: a lack of consistency in controlling variables across studies (in some cases, participants were engaged in forest bathing in indoor green spaces); a lack of insight into the longevity of the positive effects of forest bathing; and relatively small sample sizes across studies. Furthermore, some studies failed to report on whether they controlled for confounding variables such as participants' existing medication. Despite these methodological concerns, the sheer amount of data that report the beneficial outcomes of forest bathing might be seen as clear evidence of its mental health and wellbeing benefits.

Wild mindfulness

Mindfulness refers to a set of practices based to a greater or lesser extent on various forms of traditional Buddhist meditation.

Although Coleman (2010) has authored a book – *Awake in the Wild: Mindfulness in Nature as a Path of Self-Discovery* – and more recently Lymeus *et al.* (2020) found that outdoor settings can be beneficial in establishing and maintaining a state of mindfulness when compared with indoor settings, there is little literature relating to 'wild mindfulness' as a stand-alone practice.

Beyond the formal literature, internet searches return examples of wild mindfulness in practice, offered through various courses, retreats and programmes (for example, Wild Mindfulness, 2022). There is also anecdotal evidence that many other outdoor therapies include practices that have been taken, or adapted from, traditional mindfulness approaches, for example, meditation.

The lack of specific and formal literature may be due to the 'wild' prefix being relatively new, the generic and ubiquitous nature of mindfulness, and that mindfulness practices may be used extensively outdoors without being referred to as 'wild'.

3.

Discussion

As we have seen, within the vast landscape of ecotherapy there are many terms in use, or emerging. These raise some difficult semantic questions which reveal deep-seated cultural assumptions about the meaning of the words 'nature', 'therapy', 'therapeutic', 'wild' and 'wilderness', and, indeed, about the prefix, 'eco-'. Debates about this lexicon are complicated, often missed in discussion and sometimes deliberately dismissed altogether. Nevertheless, these terms, and the often-hidden assumptions that underpin them, raise critical philosophical questions. These have serious implications for ecotherapy practitioners, clients, supervisors and trainers, and, far beyond the field, for society and the rest of nature.

Philosophy can help psychology and psychotherapy with some of these metaphysical questions about how human beings conceptualize themselves within the milieu of culture, indigeneity, colonialism and hegemony. For example, questions arise such as: Are human beings and nature separate? What are the professional politics of 'therapy' and 'therapeutic'? And what is 'wild'?

This discussion uses dialectic pairs as a method to explore some of these questions, before proposing a metatheory of ecotherapy. It is hoped that, by taking a critical and broader view, a range of potentially contradictory and sometimes conflicting terms can become part of a coherent whole.

Humans and nature

Are human beings part of nature? This question is extremely complex and highly contested, mainly because of the ambiguities inherent in the word 'nature'. Within the discourse about nature, there is a wide range of definitions, which always depend on the various contexts in which the term is used, such as describing a physical space, a type of force or set of processes, or certain qualities of character. To make this more difficult, sometimes these contexts and meanings overlap. For example, a good-natured dog (characterization) might be taken for a walk in a nature reserve (place) that has been established by leaving an area of land to natural forces (process) (Ducarme & Couvet, 2020; Lewis, 1960).

A distinctive aspect of the nature narrative is that it contains numerous dualisms. These dualisms are sometimes direct, for example, the one already considered about humans and nature. Other times they are more indirect, for example, does nature include the psyche? This is really a question about whether matter includes the psyche, which in turn depends on whether nature refers to purely physical phenomena, for example, a natural area, or whether it includes metaphysical phenomena, for example, 'forces of nature' or 'natural character' or, of course, both. In brief, dualisms inherent in concepts of nature include internal and external, place and process, matter and psyche or spirit, wild and domesticated, urban and rural, nature and culture – and the classic humans and nature.

Obviously, the narrative about the meaning of nature and

the question about whether humans are part of, or separate from, it is fundamental to ecotherapy. To be clear, we would argue that human beings are part of nature, and that the notion of separation is just that: a 'notion' or an illusion which holds no ecological credibility.

One way of seeing through this illusion of separation is to attempt to site nature. Where is it? For example, is it in a forest or up a mountain? If you go 'out' into nature, where are you when you set off? In what places are you able to exist without the material contents of nature, like food, water or air – or its complexity of relational processes like pollination, transpiration or the elemental cycles of nitrogen, oxygen and carbon? At what point are we ever separate from nature? Is it even possible to exist as separate?

Where the word nature is used to describe ecotherapy practices, for example, 'nature-based therapy' and 'nature therapy', the inference is that nature is the setting for the therapy, but if, conversely, the therapy does not take place in nature, where does it take place? If everything is nature and, therefore, nature based, then all therapy is nature based and all therapy is nature therapy.

If we use the word nature loosely in an ecotherapy context, then we risk confusing the *feeling* of being disconnected psychologically from nature with literally being disconnected from it *physically*. For example, if we say that we have become 'disconnected' from nature, or that we would like to 'reconnect' to it, by implication we must believe that at times we are separate – but no distinction is ever made as to whether this separation is physical or felt. This ambiguity exacerbates the myriad problems caused by believing that we are physically separate from nature, such as unsustainable resource use and pollution. Ironically, it promotes the worldview that is leading to global-scale ecocide, worsening the very problems that many forms of ecotherapy are trying to respond to (Kidner, 2001).

Therapy and therapeutic

In Western culture, therapy, at least in the last 300 years, has been dominated by medicine and the biomedical model. The result is that, with a few radical exceptions, psychotherapy and other 'psycho' professions position themselves in relation to allopathic medicine, the medical model of diagnosis–treatment–cure, and medical health-care systems and services. This means that many Western therapies and therapists focus on disease and (psycho)pathology and, in effect, a deficit model of human experience and behaviour (one result of which is that students studying psychotherapy spend time learning psychiatric diagnostic systems). In this context, 'therapy' is sometimes juxtaposed with – and against – 'therapeutic' and then subject to territorial claims. For example, many registered psychologists and psychotherapists are happy, or at least willing, for unregistered practitioners to use the word 'therapeutic' but not the word 'therapy' or 'psychotherapist'. In this frame of reference, psychotherapy focuses on the clinical remediation of psychopathology, whereas therapeutic focuses on non-clinical, salutogenic, less well-defined and more informal practices. From this perspective, 'therapeutic' is subordinate to 'therapy'.

This hegemony is also implicit within the ecotherapy field, which is delineated along similar lines. For example, 'ecopsychotherapists' are, conventionally, accredited or registered psychotherapists who practise ecotherapy, whereas 'ecotherapists' form a more fluid group, in which some practitioners may be offering 'therapy', whereas others describe their work specifically as 'therapeutic'. Essentially, some ecotherapy practitioners might be licensed psychotherapists, others not. This distinction, and the history and politics behind it, raises important matters of practice (and the freedom to practise), regulation (statutory, professional, peer- and self-), standards and power (namely, who gets to decide these matters). Given that the environmental movement is critical and often counter-cultural and that most governments are perpetuating the ecological crises that make ecotherapy necessary in the first place, it seems somewhat ironic, as well as problematic, that ecotherapists should seek regulation, registration and recognition by the state.

Wilderness and wild

Like the word 'nature', 'wilderness' is both a frequently used and a highly contested term within ecotherapy. The contemporary, popular understanding of the word arose through the United States Wilderness Act (1964) in which wilderness is defined as 'an area where the earth and its community of life are untrammelled by man [sic], where man himself is a visitor who does not remain' (Section 2(c)). The irony is, of course, that many of the areas designated as wilderness through this Act were already home to numerous people, many of them having lived continuously in those areas for at least 10,000 years. This raises serious concerns about colonialism and indigeneity, which are shared with many other human communities living in regions defined as wilderness by colonizing white Europeans, for example, in Australia, Canada, New Zealand, South America and southern Africa. Using the term 'wilderness' in the context of ecotherapy, merely transfers these concerns, embedding the same racism and colonialism into the field and, at worst, enacting re-colonization and re-traumatization.

The etymology of the word wilderness comes from the Old English word *wilde* or *wyld*, which means 'willed' and, more specifically, 'self-willed'. This points to wilderness being more about places or situations that are not dominated or controlled by any one thing or another, whether object or subject, human or otherwise. The shift might be from 'wilderness' as a noun to 'wild' as an adjective, or arguably a verb: 'wilding'. Wildness might be experienced anywhere, rather than only in a legislated space devoid of human beings. It is a quality of experience and highly subjective, which means it cannot be designated in law.

Clearly, the debate about wilderness is not as straightforward as the contemporary use of the word would indicate and, just like with the word 'nature', 'wilderness' is often used in an ecotherapy context without a second thought to either etymology or cultural context. This makes it at best ambiguous and at worst traumatic.

Physical and metaphysical

Ecology is derived from the Greek root *oikos*, which means 'home'. Zoologist Ernst Haeckel (1876) first used the term to describe his new science of how organisms interact with their physical environment.

Ecology is all about relationships. For most people, it is about non-human organisms and how they interrelate with their habitat, but of course we humans are also organisms that interrelate with our habitat, though this might not always be 'home' (Shepherd & Woodard, 2012). The way anything interrelates with its environment is complicated. In physical terms alone, the web of complexity often exceeds our capacity to understand it. There is constant novel emergence: we discover new and surprising connections all the time, just when we think we have worked everything out.

A common assumption is that ecology is only physical. However, what about all the metaphysical relationships organisms have with their environment? Most humans experience emotional, creative, spiritual, intuitive, psychological and social relationships with their environment, as well as physical ones. Different environments have different meanings to different people. These impact how we interrelate with our environment – and how our environment shapes our sense of self and, therefore, our psychology. Although we cannot speak for other species, there is no burden of proof to suggest that they do not share similar metaphysical relationships too.

Thus, when and wherever the prefix 'eco-' is used, it must account for this wildly broad and deep, physical and metaphysical ecology.

Culture and indigeneity

In therapy, as in life, there are great debates about culture and the meaning of culture, especially as it relates to identity. Although everyone has a culture, this term has often been used to refer to others, thereby posing a central and supposedly neutral (and predominantly white) cultural norm, with the decentred other ('Other') being marginalized – and either exoticized or demonized. Fortunately (from the authors' point of view), critical theory has helped shift thinking in therapy from a focus on multiculturalism and multicultural competencies (which tends to focus on understanding the other but ultimately maintains 'them' at the margins) to that on 'cultural intentionality' (Shweder, 1990) and deconstructing notions of hegemonic culture such as whiteness (Applebaum, 2016; Giroux, 1997). In this process, the literature on indigeneity has been crucial.

One mechanism and process in this field is the assimilation of the cultural other, for example, through explicit colonial policies of erasing indigeneity through 'breeding [it] out' (Robyn-Rapsey, 2013). One example of this in this field is the assimilation of terms such as 'shamanism', 'yoga' and 'mindfulness', all of which have become homogenized in contemporary culture in ways that sever them from their specific cultural and spiritual origins. Their use is rarely sanctioned for dissemination into other cultural contexts by those with the authority to do so (Jones & Segal, 2018). Many of those teaching and promoting these practices outside the culture in which they originated are not steeped in that culture and have not completed the culturally appropriate training to become a 'master' of these practices. Used in contemporary culture and especially in the West, both shamanism and mindfulness often homogenize extremely diverse, highly sophisticated and intensely contextual ancient practices into over-simplified and shallow concepts. Such assimilation, especially in the hands of privileged white people, appears as another form of colonization, and thus represents a further insult to, and re-traumatization of, those from whose cultures they are taken, that is, stolen. Finally, the fact that these practices are then usually commercialized is particularly insensitive and deeply ironic if not cynical, given that global consumer capitalism was the cause of the destruction of many of these original practices and the traditions in which they were embedded, during the colonizing expansionism of post-Renaissance Europe (Jones & Segal, 2018).

Skin-bound self and ecological Self

Concepts of self are central to all psychological discourse and, despite distinct and sometimes competing views, many modalities share the same or similar definitions. The most common conception of self in contemporary psychology can be represented by the 'skin-bound ego' (Anzieu, 1989; see also Berne, 1961). This is the self that is contained within or by the physical body: it is the one that we usually understand when we refer to 'me', 'myself' or 'I'. This notion of selfhood is the apotheosis of the individualism deeply embedded in the Western philosophical tradition. It forms the basis of a society that comprises a collection of separate individuals interrelating through a complex web of psychosocial interactions. Individualism is also, of course, the very foundation of classic economic theory and contemporary political and social science. Curiously, what is conventionally referred to as 'nature' is absent from most contemporary psychological narratives on selfhood. Factoring it into these narratives is the primary rationale of ecopsychology, as we have found.

The absence of nature from psychology was first identified philosophically by Arne Næss, emeritus professor of philosophy at the University of Oslo during the early 1970s. Around this time, environmental ethics were beginning to enter public discourse through Carson's (1965) seminal text *Silent Spring* and the emergence of legal narratives about the rights of nature, for example, in Stone's (1972) revolutionary essay on the legal standing of trees. These catalysed the field of ecological philosophy, later termed 'ecosophy' by Næss (1989). Næss had a strong interest in psychology borne of an intense period of psychoanalysis that he undertook with Edward Hitschmann, a personal colleague of Sigmund Freud, and through his involvement with the Vienna Circle, both while a student at the University of Vienna (Fox, 1992). This transdisciplinary interest led him to use a philosophical frame of reference based on widening fields of ethical 'concern', to propose an ecological definition of self:

> Traditionally the maturity of the self develops through three stages – from ego to social self, and from social self to metaphysical self. In this conception of the process, nature – our home, our immediate environment, where we belong as children, and our identification with living beings – is largely ignored. I therefore tentatively introduce the concept of an ecological Self.
>
> (Næss, 1995, p. 226)

As already noted, the ecological 'Self' was capitalized by Næss to distinguish it from the narrower skin-bound 'self' of conventional psychology. From this perspective, 'nature' includes both physical and metaphysical phenomena – and human beings.

These two ideas of selfhood form a polarity, with the skin-bound 'humans are separate from nature' self on one side and the ecological 'humans are part of nature' self on the other. Clearly, any ecotherapy practice based on the former idea of self is not 'eco-' therapy at all.

4.

Metatheory

It is clear from the findings in Chapter 2 that the contemporary nomenclature of ecotherapy and ecopsychology is insufficient: it is not adequate, congruent or accurate. There is no satisfactory way to categorize ecotherapy or ecopsychology using terms such as nature therapy, outdoor yoga, shamanic practice, wilderness therapy or wild mindfulness, for example. In every case, these terms have been interpreted differently, depending on the practitioners using them. The challenges of semantics, conflicting assumptions about selfhood, as well as the unclear delineation between physical and metaphysical phenomena, make a cohesive and complete naming of different approaches to ecotherapy and ecopsychology impossible. Indeed, it is only by abandoning the desire to organize practices by name that any useful taxonomy can emerge. We need a broader vision for making sense of this field.

In order to do this, we have formulated a metatheory that transcends the specific names given by practitioners to their work. This is based on two axes, which form four distinct paradigms. All the fields and practices that we have explored can be organized into these paradigms, regardless of the specific terms used.

The x-axis represents a continuum from anthropocentric (human as therapist) to ecocentric (nature as therapist). The y-axis represents the continuum from reciprocal (humans are

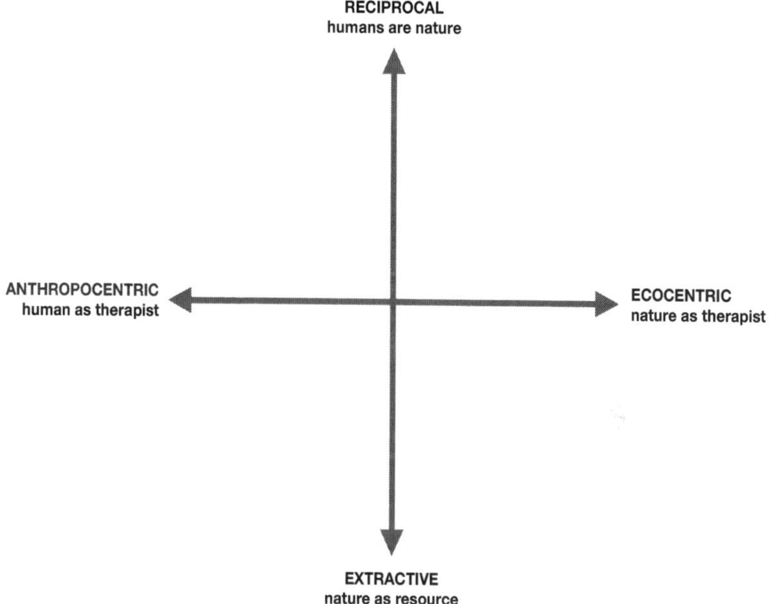

Figure 4.1. *Ecotherapy paradigms*

nature) to extractive (nature as resource). As such, both are ontological: the *x*-axis describes the essence of therapy, whereas the *y*-axis describes the essence of nature.

The anthropocentric (human as therapist) paradigm assumes that the human therapist is primary and the therapeutic process is centred in their modality, the frameworks they use, their training, experience and their technique. Everything is understood from the perspective of the individual human, whether therapist, client or another human protagonist. The assumption is made that human concerns should, and do, have priority over those of any other living being.

The ecocentric (nature as therapist) paradigm assumes

that nature – including but not privileging the therapist, the client and other human beings – is primary, and that the therapeutic process is sited within a vast and diffuse ecological field. Everything is understood from a relational, ecological perspective.

The extractive paradigm (nature as resource) assumes that nature is a resource to be used purely for providing therapeutic human experiences. The reciprocal paradigm (humans are nature) assumes that human beings exist in reciprocity with their wider, nested ecosystems, as an integral part of them.

This metatheory avoids the pitfalls of creating a taxonomy of labels for different practices of ecotherapy. Crucially, we argue that many of the practices reviewed can be placed in *any* of the quadrants, depending on the practitioner's view of therapy and nature. For instance, a therapist could practise adventure therapy, forest bathing, forest therapy, nature-based therapy or wild therapy in any of the four paradigms, based on their assumptions about nature and their own role in the therapeutic process.

One aspect that is less subjective, however, is that the respective anthropocentric/extractive paradigm set and the ecocentric/reciprocal paradigm set are based on fundamentally opposing principles. Drawing on the metaphor of a line in the sand, Figure 4.2 clarifies this opposition through the addition of a 'line of ecological contradiction'. This sharply delineates different practices based on their underlying assumptions. Whether or not the choice is deliberate in the same way that inaction is a form of action, as a practitioner you work on either one side of the line or the other. What defines this line is the use of ecology as a unifying concept. Any term that uses the word 'ecology' or the prefix 'eco-' makes sense only on the ecocentric/reciprocal side of the line, because anthropocentric and extractive approaches can never be valid or justified from an ecological point of view.

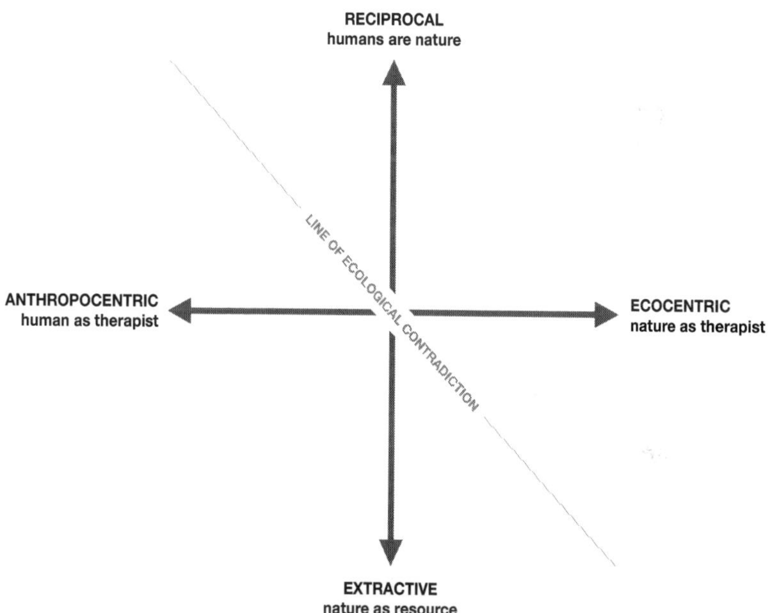

Figure 4.2. *Ecotherapy paradigms and the line of ecological contradiction*

Of course, the principles underlying this metatheory are not new. Within the Western tradition, they are intrinsic to the 'shallow' and 'deep' formulations of deep ecology (Næss,

1973) and can be traced at least as far back as Leopold's (1949) land ethic. Within Indigenous cultures, they can be traced back over millennia. Similar concepts have been explored within ecotherapy and ecopsychology contexts specifically, but not as part of a distinct metatheory (e.g. Conn & Conn, 2009; DeMayo, 2009; Fisher, 2013a). Key identified these principles in his ecotherapy professional development programmes in the mid-2000s, characterizing therapy (t) as comprising 'little "t"' and 'big "T"' approaches. These correspond to the anthropocentric/extractive and ecocentric/reciprocal paradigms (Figure 4.2), respectively. However, this type of distinction first appeared in a formal publication some ten years later. Buzzell (2016), for example, refers specifically to 'Level 1' and 'Level 2' approaches – anthropocentric/extractive and ecocentric/reciprocal in our metatheory. However, she also suggests that there is a continuum of practice that is ill-defined, writing that 'Many ecotherapies – probably most – can be practised at either Level 1 or Level 2 or somewhere along the scale between them' (p. 73). Of course, we would argue that any practice is, by definition, either ecological (ecocentric/reciprocal) or not (anthropocentric/extractive) and that describing a non-ecological approach as 'ecotherapy' is, in fact, simply wrong. The problem arises when approaches are generically referred to as 'ecotherapies', which takes us full circle back to the tricky semantics and taxonomy that our metatheory aims to resolve.

Ultimately, this metatheory invites people to think philosophically about practice. We have already suggested that the axes themselves represent statements about ontology, or the essence of things. Next, we say a bit more about this as well as two other philosophical areas of enquiry, regarding axiology (ethics or values) and epistemology (theories of knowledge). We suggest that thinking more philosophically about practice and striving for greater philosophical congruence – that is, of personal philosophy, the philosophy of a particular approach and practice (Tudor & Worrall, 2006) – enables the practitioner to strengthen their understanding, their practice and how they represent themselves to both clients and colleagues.

Ontology

Ontology presents practitioners with questions about their understanding of the essence of nature and their being as a therapist. Are we part of nature or is it – an *it* – a set of objects and processes separate from us? Is nature only physical or does it include metaphysical phenomena? Considering these questions exposes assumptions that are deeply rooted in cultural norms and personal experiences. Without needing to provide a full analysis of these norms, any of them can be tested against ecological reality, that is to say that our reality is beyond and, indeed, despite us. If people were eradicated from the face of the earth, something would still exist. Something existed before us and will exist after we have gone. This something is the basis of all human subjectivism, the *prima materia* of every human concept and, like the famous silent falling tree in the Zen tradition, whether or not we are there to experience it, it still exists.

The true test of this 'ontological realism' in an ecological context is absolute and empirical (Næss, 1975). We cannot exist without our ecosystems; our ecosystems, however, can exist, in one form or another, without us. This challenges the anthropocentric and separatist ontology of industrial growth culture entirely, because it has no ecologically sound basis. Another way of understanding the ecology of ontological realism is through Gestalt ontology, which holds that not only is the whole greater than the sum of its parts, but also the part is greater as a result of its whole. Thus, the human experience of a tree depends not only on the tree itself plus any preconceived ideas, cultural norms, memories of and desires about trees, but also on the ecological context of the tree. A tree in a wild forest is experienced differently from a tree on a city street, in a garden or an arboretum. Whatever a tree is to a human being is based on both internal and external, and physical and metaphysical phenomena (Diehm, 2006; Næss, 1989). Given that ecotherapy is by definition 'eco-', that is to say ecological, whether practitioners embrace or reject an ecological ontology is fundamental to the congruence and efficacy of their practice.

As soon as an ecological ontology is accepted, the person and role of the therapist are radically changed. In most, if not all, therapeutic modalities, the client, the therapist and their relationship to each other are the main sites of the therapeutic process. Wherever the focus and emphasis may be at any one time, these three figures – client, therapist and their relationship – usually hold the process. But what happens when we change the focus from this human relational field to the wider context in which it exists? What happens when we think about the essence of things far beyond the human social field? What if the actual therapeutic potential lies in the complex web of relationships with everything, not just between the microcosm of client and therapist and their relationship? The original research that is often cited as supporting the importance of the therapeutic relationship on the outcome of psychotherapy (Lambert, 1992) also reveals that 40 per cent of change in clients is attributable to extra-therapeutic factors. Although the author was not focusing on any particular form of therapy, he did refer to 'the natural helping systems that are abundant in the environment' (Lambert, 1992, p. 99). In this case, if the therapist, as the one curating the therapy, privileges themselves over any other source of relationship, then they effectively get in the way of the therapeutic process. An ecological ontology demands that the ecotherapist takes a vastly different role from the usual, traditional form, which we can think about as a two-person-plus psychology (Tudor, 2011).

Axiology

In addition to ontological questions about the essence of nature and the role of the therapist, the way that nature is valued and the dynamics of power and hegemony between humans and the rest of nature form an important axiological narrative.

Næss (1993) argues that nature has intrinsic value, which lies beyond its usefulness to human beings. That nature's only value is to be found when it is externalized into some separate, purely human domain, provides the opposite position. Of course, if humans are understood as being part of the rest of nature, then this latter position is nonsense, as there is no external domain. In the metatheory then, the extractive paradigm assumes nature only holds extrinsic value, whereas the reciprocal one is synonymous with it having intrinsic value.

Important power dynamics arise between the anthropocentric and ecocentric paradigms. On the one hand, humans are regarded as rightfully having absolute power and moral authority over the rest of nature. On the other, this authority requires a form of human exceptionalism that is morally unacceptable and ecologically dangerous. For example, believing that humans should have the authority to exert power over the rest of nature has led to ecological crises, and moral and ethical dilemmas, on a planetary scale

From this perspective, a number of concepts need revision. For instance, while also implying responsibilities and duties of care that align with an ecocentric paradigm, stewardship allots human beings the role of dominion over the rest of nature, which is deeply anthropocentric. The concept of custodianship is similar but more ecocentric, as it suggests taking responsibility without assuming a power dynamic of control or dominion. Biocentric equality refers to the equal rights of all forms of life. The content of these rights varies according to cultural norms; for example, in European cultures, dogs and cats are kept as pets and are considered 'more equal' than chickens and cows, which are farmed and killed to be eaten. This can also be seen within the environmental movement through the wildly asymmetrical allocation of resources to conserving 'charismatic megafauna', especially mammals, over other life forms such as spiders, snakes, fish or fungi. Distinct axiological decisions are made here, albeit under the wide umbrella of biocentrism. Another challenge with biocentrism is that, technically, it refers only to life forms ('bio') and excludes the systems and processes that support them ('eco'). The term ecocentric equality resolves this, as, by definition, ecology is a relational and therefore an inclusive term.

Leopold (1949, p. 224) provides an important touchstone for ecocentric ethics in his seminal essay 'The Land Ethic', in which he states, 'A thing is right when it tends to preserve the integrity, stability, and beauty of the biotic community. It is wrong when it tends otherwise'. He goes on to write that this ethic extends the concept of community and, 'changes the role of *Homo sapiens* from conqueror of the land-community to plain member and citizen of it' (p. 204). This ethic is obviously positioned within an ecocentric/reciprocal paradigm and is stunning in its foresight, acuity and ecological validity in the Western context, given when it was published.

Axiologically, then, life forms and the processes that support them share intrinsic value in an ecological context. Human beings are not exceptional or external, as they are subject to precisely the same ecological processes – and limitations – of any other living thing. Meanwhile, a belief in dominion and control over nature is just that: a belief. Although there is no doubt that we humans can exert power over the rest of nature, there is much evidence that this is ecocidal, let alone morally indefensible. The reason why it is ecocidal, of course, is because in the long term we cannot really dominate or control the rest of nature at all. Like Daniel

Quinn's (1995) famous metaphor of falling being mistaken for flying, human domination of, and control over, the rest of nature are myths: eventually the ground will be encountered. The reason it is morally indefensible is because it privileges the rights of some over their responsibilities to others, thus limiting the rights of those others. As an ecotherapy practitioner, these axiological continuums, paradoxes and positions all inform practice, whether consciously or not. They all also fall, one way or another, either side of the line of ecological contradiction.

Epistemology

Whether philosophers or practitioners think first about the essence of things (ontology) or ethics and values (axiology), both inform how we know things. Put simply, if we think of ourselves as independent, thinking individuals, we will look to our rational minds for what we know (that is, the truth is in here), if we regard ourselves as subjects of some superordinate being, we will look outside ourselves, for example, to religion for our values and what we know (the truth is out there) and, if we regard ourselves as fundamentally relational beings, we will tend to rely on our relationships with others (human or otherwise) for our understanding (the truth is in the in-between). Thus, if we wish to be philosophically congruent, it is important that our theory or theories of knowledge align with our theories about being and values.

Kahn and Hasbach (2012) identify five main orientations or perspectives – in other words, theories of knowledge – that have shaped the field of ecopsychology: the ecological unconscious, phenomenology, the interconnectedness of all beings and Gaia theory, the transpersonal and the transcendental (the last two we consider together) (Table 4.1).

Perspectives in ecopsychology (Kahn & Hasbach, 2012)	**Focus**	**Authors**
Ecological unconscious	On repression, mental illness, irrationality, ego identification	Shepard (1982), Roszak (1992)
Phenomenology	On direct experience of the natural, physical and human world, and the text	Kohak (1984), Abram (1996)
The inter-connectedness of all beings, Gaia theory	On the inseparability of self, other, object and nature	Lovelock (1972), Næss (1989)
The transpersonal The transcendental	On the idea that interaction with nature helps provide for optimal mental health, including spiritual, mystical and others 'across' or 'beyond' experiences	Davis (2011), Jung (1968, 1989), Snyder (2010)

Table 4.1. *Perspectives in ecopsychology*

To take the example of the ecological unconscious (e.g. Kerr & Key, 2012), we can know this through different forms of enquiry (such as self-reflection, conversation, group therapy and so on), and we can research it by means of different methods (heuristic, autoethnographic, case study, etc.), all of which are informed by different theories (hermeneutics, grounded theory, etc.), for a summary of which see Table 4.2.

Perspectives in ecopsychology (Kahn & Hasbach, 2012)	**Research methods**	**Research methodologies**
Ecological unconscious Phenomenology The interconnectedness of all beings, Gaia theory The transpersonal The transcendental	Case study Conversation analysis Discourse analysis Focus groups Heuristic Interpretation Interview Literature review Narrative analysis Participant observation Questionnaire Thematic analysis	Critical race theory Critical theory Deep ecology Ethnography Feminism Hermeneutics Heuristic Grounded theory Phenomenology

Table 4.2 *Perspectives in ecopsychology with examples of research methods and methodologies*

All the perspectives noted in Tables 4.1 and 4.2 represent theories of knowledge that are reciprocal and ecological and, therefore, on the right side (in both senses of the word) of the line of ecological contradiction. We think this is a particularly important point to make because some forms of ecotherapy, as currently presented and practised, sit clearly on the extractive/anthropocentric side of this line. However, ecopsychology and its practice through ecotherapy have, from their inception, always been based on reciprocal and ecocentric epistemologies. We hope that our metatheory provides an opportunity for practitioners to honour this heritage.

In summary, this metatheory provides a clear map that helps track through the ontology, axiology and epistemology of the vast and complex field that is ecotherapy. Despite the inherent complexity of the field, we suggest that overlaying principles of ecology, which lie at the heart of ecopsychology and ecotherapy, delineates a clear line between fundamentally conflicting approaches. This line has serious implications for how practitioners choose to describe and practise their work, if they are to do so ethically, accurately and effectively.

5.

Reflections and responses

with Dion Enari, Rebecca Freeth, Rupert Hutchinson, Hayley Marshall, Jacoba Matapo, Gina O'Neill and Bianca Stawiarski

This chapter comprises five pieces from seven colleagues – from Aotearoa New Zealand, Australia, Samoa, South Africa and the United Kingdom – whom we invited to contribute their responses to this book. These are followed by our reflections on their responses.

We have been careful to invite a very broad diversity of perspectives, especially from Indigenous peoples and from those whom some might feel are not ecotherapists at all, mainly because they are not clinical psychologists or psychotherapists. We want to challenge the idea that ecotherapy is a form of psychotherapy. Being outside is intrinsically healing. Working with that potential consciously can be done in many ways, by very different people in extremely diverse contexts, towards a wide range of outcomes. All the people whom we have invited fall into this category; they all engage professionally, one way or another, with the therapeutic power of nature.

Obviously, inviting responses to what we have written and then offering our own reflections are just two steps along a much longer conversational path. Our hope here is to contribute to, and help stimulate, an evolving dialogue. We do not aim to attempt the impossible, pointless and undesirable task of trying to 'pin things down' or, in the age-old philosophical tradition, establish 'a position'. This means that any issues raised in these contributions, as well as any differences and tensions between them, remain open.

Responses

Wiru and wairua

Gina Marie O'Neill and Bianca F. Stawiarski

On invitation from Keith and Dave in Aotearoa, each of us separately sat with Country from our different cultural experiences as First Nations women, connected with the Country that we were sitting on, while also connecting to our own countries and lands we come from. We deeply listened, observed, waited, sensed and connected as we read the book. This is our response that comes out of that. In order to maintain the flow of this contribution but also to make it accessible, we provide (at the end) a glossary of words used in the Badimaya/Badimia and Māori languages.

Ngardi guwanda …
Sitting on barna, I reach both around me and within.
Barna calls, caresses and heals.
The wind blows both across my body and through me.
Reminding me of who I am.

Surrounded by life, ancestors and ceremony,
Of Kaurna land that I am but a visitor on.
The bird song on the breeze,

The hum of the little creatures,
The rustle in the leaves,
The spirits everywhere.

I breathe with Barna,
Feeling a shift in who I am,
Ngaliming wiru dhadhadyabaya.

Connection with Barna is not new,
Our people have always healed in this way.
It is time that our voices are fully heard,
That we move connection to Barna back outside the walls and outside the medical journals.

It is with joy I hear the cry in these pages for a recognition,
Of our healing ways to be honoured.
That Barna be more than a backdrop to the healing of ourselves and our communities.

Barna heals, barna resources, and soothes.
Combined with a skilled healer or therapist,
Barna is a powerful connection of transformation,
And for that, ngalimi yunggudya.

Barna doesn't need labels.
People need labels, and this book opens this discussion.
It needs to go further though …
Ecopsychology or ecotherapy forgets spirit, ignores ancestors.

There needs to be a deep honouring of the mabarn,
In Barna, in ourselves, in ancestors singing.
Let's together explore the naming of this practice,
Where the therapy is untamed, deep and expansive.

There must be an acknowledgement, a recognition,
Of the pain of place …
The deep wounding that Barna may have experienced or witnessed
That there are places of sickness,
That need to be healed before any healing can occur there.

The tears from Ranginui is the rain falling down to Papatūānuku. These tears of separation, grief and pain are also nurturing and caring, creating the waters of the rivers and oceans that give life and healing.
Arakwal, Gadigal, Kahungunu and Rangitane, Yahweh and aroha.

Calling in wairua
Listen, listen to kōkōhau
I am with manu.

How do we see each other as moana does in her power? Worldview of non-Western peoples? What about te Ao non-Indigenous?
Country heals and our practices work together with the land with Papatūānuku: we heal together.

Calling in wairua
Listen, listen to kōkōhau
I am with Papatūānuku.

I can see what you cannot see so easily from where I sit.
Kōkōhau brushes over moana.
We can see what you cannot see so easily from where we are.
We see how things work from where we are.
How can we see both of our ways to heal as equals at the therapy table? We don't need to be the same; we need to listen and understand Western and Indigenous ways for what each of them brings to therapy and healing in different ways – there's no need to Westernize.

Breathe,
My lungs in me and my lungs in taiao,
The practice of slowing, resting, breathing with is us and we are her;
I know my place here, I have what I need here and I gift this also to her.
The goal of healing is to restore balance – two-way together – connection to the kookaburras and blue tongues; wind restores balance.

Calling in wairua
Listen, listen to kōkōhau
I am with ancestors.

> Tinana, hinengaro, wairua, whenua and whānau,
> inseparable
> The sun warms my skin – settle, pause, find the balance.
> A therapist holds this space with the sun, where all is
> natural – the anger, the rage, the hurt – whenua knows
> this pain – the compassion, the joy, the laughing –
> whenua knows this love.
> Time stands still in this work; then everything is
> possible and abundant.
>
> Individual, separate, science competing, prove it.
> Wait! Listen! Rustling in that bush over there, my kin
> warning me.
> Come back, remember and reconnect to ancestors and
> country/whenua – you are not a label, we do not label, a
> starting place not to be fixed or sorted.
>
> Two crow brothers, their oily black blue feathers, not
> afraid, walking with strength and character:
> 'We know what we are doing', 'We know what we are
> about', 'Don't fear'.

As Badimaya and Māori, we used our shared connection to Country and place, our deep understanding and honouring of ancestors and spirit to explore the approaches and definitions in this book. When on Country, the Westernized concepts, and definitions of what we do and what to call this practice seem so misplaced and encompass only a tiny part of what this practice is. When we as First Nations healers try to

Glossary

(of non-English words in the order in which they appear)

In the Badimaya/Badimia language

wiru – spirit
ngardi guwanda – deep listening
barna – land
Barna – Country
ngaliming wiru dhadhadyabaya – our spirit is getting strong
ngalimi yunggudya – we give to each other
mabarn – medicine

In te reo Māori (the Māori language)

wairua – spirit
Ranginui – Sky father
Papatūānuku – Earth mother
Kahungunu – a tribe of Aotearoa
Rangitane – a sub-tribe of Aotearoa
aroha – love
kōkōhau – breeze
manu – muttonbird
moana – the sea
te Ao – the world/worldview
taiao – the natural world/nature
tinana – physiological health/wellbeing
hinengaro – mind
whenua – land
whānau – family

In the Bundjalung language

Yahweh – thank you

People

Kaurna – the people of the Adelaide plains
Arakwal – a tribe of the Bundjalung Nation
Gadigal – a tribe of the Eora Nation

explore what could be the right word for what we do, we come up short. How can you give name to the intricate nature of the breeze? Of our very real experience of feeling ancestors of place, of the beings in the trees. How can we describe a word to fully describe internal parts of people talking with the beings in trees? Ecotherapy or ecopsychology seems to be such a simplified two-dimensional concept for a place, a space that is non-linear, timeless, physical and spiritual. What we have attempted to do is to describe what Country shows to us as we explore the definitions in this book. We believe that this book is an incredible, important opportunity to start the yarn on what this could be, not what people before us have suggested this is. It is exciting that through this book we now know all the words that this is not. This can only be discovered when we fully open ourselves to listen deeply to Country. Let us come together to explore what this could be. We extend our hands to you all to enter this yarn.

We are the land and seas, and they are us

Jacoba Matapo and Dion Enari

As we explore ecotherapy and other forms of therapeutic practice, we can see it informed by an individual's relationship with the natural environment. As this field of scholarship grows in this area, a constant question we ask is how can we make sense of the field of ecotherapy? As a daughter and son of the Islands of Samoa now residing in Aotearoa, we believe the answer to this is through our Pacific ways of being and knowing. Indigenous Pacific conceptualizations of Moana

(Pacific Ocean) as home extend the sense of belonging and identity among Pacific peoples to include lands and waters (Hau'ofa, 2008). Pacific peoples share an affinity with Moana, as historically Moana navigators used the wind, rhythm, tides, sea currents, sun, moon, stars, clouds and birds to navigate paths into the known and unknown. For Pacific peoples, Moana generates personal and collective connections (Matapo & Baice, 2020). The life force of Moana (that is, its capacities) interplays with the cosmos and creation and has been storied extensively in the epistemologies of Pacific peoples. Epeli Hau'ofa (2008), a Tongan scholar, argues that it is critical for Pacific peoples to resist the restrictive nature of hegemonic views that present Pacific Islands as 'small'. He boldly claims: 'We are the sea, we are the ocean, we must wake up to this ancient truth and together use it to overturn all hegemonic views that aim ultimately to confine us again, physically and psychologically, in the tiny spaces' (Hau'ofa, 2008, p. 39).

We are the land and seas, and they are us,
So, why the need for ecotherapy?
The great nature/culture divide.
As if humans could separate from nature.
Economics and politics
The hierarchy of being
Internalized capitalism
Privileged metaphysics
Ontologies of difference
Kinship metaphysics
Relational ontologies with world

Nature–culture kinship
Co-agentic and co-evolutionary:
Ecological ties to being and becoming.

Theories of the culture/nature divide centred upon dualisms are prevalent in the Western philosophical tradition and present nature as something non-agentic to be tamed. The properties of nature are not humanistic; therefore, they do not have the same agentic capacity, specifically logic or reason. It seems that complicity with capitalism and the exploitation of the natural world renders nature a standing reserve for 'man' and, therefore, available for exploitation. Earth or nature in Western philosophy discourse continues to present this position of the 'world' as an object for the benefit and use of humans, where the exploitation of natural energies is fundamental to modern technologies (Heidegger, 1977). It is from this position of 'lack' that nature is presented as inert. The instrumental rationality of science produced factions between nature and the human subject position and, at the time of modernity, was a critical feature of social domination. From an Indigenous Samoan position, we propose a different metaphysical perspective, a co-evolutionary position that draws from Samoan cosmogony and gagana (language). Tui Atua (2014) describes the Samoan creation story, the genesis of land, skies, seas, human life and sentient and non-sentient beings. The naming of the body in gagana Samoa reflects the metaphysical relationship between human and non-human life:

> Man is God-descended, and there are genealogical links between the sun, the moon, the seas, the rocks, the earth … earth and all living organisms, including human, originated from a 'big bang', the tumultuous separation of Lagi (heaven) and Papa (rock) … Following the separation … god Tagaloa sent his messenger Tuli (plover) to Papa to help create plants and trees. Tuli is also attributed with discovering and germinating the lands of Samoa, Tonga and Fiji. Tuli, on Tagaloa's instructions, then designated the human form from ilo (bacteria that became maggots). Samoans named the ankle tuli vae and the elbow tuli lima in recognition of the work of Tuli.
>
> (Tui Atua, 2014, p. 16)

As we explore the Samoan language more, we can see how the environment is us and we are the environment. The Samoan word fanua means both earth and placenta, the Samoan word to/ko means to plant and to be pregnant. All Samoan oratory speeches also make reference to the environment through acknowledging the skies, seas and mountains that surround and sustain them.

We ask how does an understanding of Samoan relational ecologies provide insights into non-dualistic notions of wellbeing? As Samoan people, our islands are literally our mother(land) (Enari & Viliamu Jameson, 2021). We reject the Eurocentric hierarchical notion of 'man' being above all; instead, we acknowledge that we are the land and the sea, and the land and sea are us (Matapo, 2021; Matapo & Enari, 2021). Today, as her offspring, many of us devote our lives to her protection and conservation. As Samoans, we believe that, if the people take care of the environment, the environment will take care of the people – and remember, if the land and seas are well, so are the people.

Axis

Hayley Marshall

I stand,
an innocent adrift,
on a wave of autumn crisp bracken.
Wren pierce their warning,
throwing me out.
Every 'here' is someone's place.
I am big,
I am too much.
The wrong shape,
measured in the wrong way,
in the wrong position.
Where,
do I put myself?

A response sounds from the overstanding.
Large birds arriving, one buzzard, then two.
Stooping low into woodland, they press glides of
authority through tree-tight spaces, barely enough for a
raptor wingspan.
Their navigation is artful, impressive,

a self-willed majesty, free of jurisdiction, guided only by
a line of wild.
With an immense sweep of magic
these overstory lords spirit me
across to move with tall pine.
Washed through with awe,
I am eclipsed.
Place, graced by bird,
is blessed.
It doesn't need me to be here,
I am small,
I am of no consequence.
I again fall backwards,
into a pool of narcissism,
of human redundancy.
What,
Is the point of me?

My movement becomes limp and aimless,
Until cronk of raven,
psychopomp with dark echo,
drops me to earth.
This!
This, is the necessary gesture.
I bury my face,
press my animal nose into layered ground,
and breathe,
and breathe.
I breathe earth and they breathe me.

I surrender to reciprocal flow,
a rolling affinity between soil and
tree-lunged core of creaturely body.
Riding this wave of inspiration,
I am taken.
Swept away on olfactory wings
to fermented heartlands,
spreading traces of time past,
I descend perfumed horizons of this understanding.
Through vapour of sweet menthol surface,
into sharp song of marshed moss,
beyond cave-aged tang of bark,
cascading to ancient pools,
beetle holding court
in the stinging bile of a digestive deep.
Now,
I become a true earth traveller,
seasoned witness to other realms.

In these depths, I surface,
I reach for what's here,
I am earth,
I am animal,
I am soul.

I am human,
sacred,
bowing and praying.
I am lived,

and only now,
am I
placed.

Commentary

I agree with David and Keith's premise that how we use words is very important, and that where they come from in us is a significant consideration – but I want to emphasize that we need to shift our ways of sourcing them significantly. This affects how we conceptualize our position in the world generally, and also in our practice. As in the poem, my sense is that we need to connect to the earth through our animal, moving, sensing body and find our axes from there. The words that arise from the earthed-body are different from ones arising just from a human intellectual process. They offer ecological sense.

Therefore, my initial response to David and Keith's words is offered in a form that reflects my own personal and professional ecological practice. I have been going out to make communion with places near my home in Derbyshire, United Kingdom, for many years now. This supports my sense of being-well in the world, which I know arises from an affinity with the more-than-human.

The practice is centred in the Amerta movement (Bloom *et al.*, 2014) and a synaesthesic sensory connection with the natural world. It involves a gradual melting into the smell, taste and movement of the place: essentially a sensual erotic process of unselfing (Murdoch, 1970), honouring a human porosity to the earth. Through this, I offer my somatic attention to a place to discover the wisdom that is held there, to 'hear' the messages for me as a human animal. I craft the words arising into a written piece that creates its own creaturely form – usually prose-poetry – often offering a distinct ecological message. Finally, in a gesture of reciprocity, I offer my words back to the place, honouring the teachings.

More recently, I have been sharing some of this work with wider audiences through performance, writing and education. As a result, I understand that the process has relevance for addressing the wider issue of how we as a human species find a new way of speaking, as humans living among other forms of animate life.

The practice is now the way I respond to most things in my life, especially if I want to find wider and deeper wisdom. So, naturally, I bring David and Keith's writing out to my local land, Lightwood – a patch of open-access land on the edge of the town where I live.

Before moving in this place, I think of how important it is to cultivate receiving before responding. Positionality is key here. With so many different lenses involved in offering and receiving, I take time to absorb where David and Keith speak from.

Now I feel it important to calibrate my own lens of receiving, some sense of where their words are landing. I am a white, middle-class woman, a university-educated psychotherapist based in the northern hemisphere. This offers some sense of my identity but not of my wider personhood – the lands I am *of*. The poem offers some glimpse of this place forming part of my sense of self. This is my symmathesy (Bateson, 2016), where 'me' is a dynamic, human-nuanced process incorporating the more-than-human.

All of this affects how and what I receive, *and* experience tells me that I (and others) receive words differently outside with the land, among the agency of the more-than-human. Through the practice described above, I open to the mind (intelligence) of the land. I settle into my place in the scheme of things and then listen. I then write to David and Keith from there.

This is *how* my response words come and this, in my opinion, is where most of our human words need to come from – the ground-human-up, not the human-top-down.

The scoping clarity David and Keith bring to the labels that abound in outdoor and ecological practice reminds me of the whirlwind of confusion that can ensue in a human-top-down world. This wrestle with terminology is so familiar to me. In my early days as an outdoor practitioner in the UK, I remember countless campfire 'discussions' about many of the terms they explore. This felt like entering a very angry hornets' nest full of passion in the fight for territory. A diverse group of practitioners meeting in the essential liminality of outdoor places, we were locked in with our search for the categorical – 'How do I name who I am? What I do? Who are you? What are you doing? What do I call all of this?'

As we entered this existential uncertainty with its dark clouds of fear, we stalled on losing the foothold of status. Unlike hornets (I imagine!), we never got anywhere satisfying, and I often felt that something was missing. Now I can see that this was because we (in those discussions) were engaged in a typical Western human approach, that is, attempting to answer these and many other questions in isolation from the more-than-human. We were still in our human echo chamber. All of the questions involved asking only the human for answers; significantly, no one asked, '*Where* am I?' as a starting point. We were adrift, without integrity, apart from our more-than-human relatives.

I like David and Keith's metatheory – it is clear and elegant, inviting practitioners to work from their philosophical ground in relation to the earth. Aligned with the ground-human-up, I encourage the people I train to find this ground literally. I emphasize: the importance of a personal ecological practice for the practitioner so they can work out who they are in relationship with the land; what the earth calls them to be; what they want to do from there; and, only then, what they might name themselves to the human world. For a typical Western person, this involves challenging inner and outer work, a considerable ecological journey to become embedded ecological citizens.

We *are* nature, but, in the Western mind, that can still just remain an intellectual idea unless we actually engage with the 'outside', particularly the living-outside, otherwise we remain interiorized. Moving beyond this has to be an *embodied* relational endeavour, of somatically knowing that our human 'I' is among others, and that the ecological self is a phenomenological reality.

As practitioners, if we receive others from this perspective – from wren, buzzard, raven, fermented earth, beetle – we can develop new ways of hearing the people we work with. With these other forms of living offering us their different knowings, we may then reach for different/new words to bring to the work of the soul. The language arising is rooted, often poetic, speaking the truths of earth-soul-sacred.

Over my time working in connection with the earth, I have learnt the immense value of shedding human categories in order to discover more-than-human knowings. This, in the world of the old stories (Shaw, 2021), would be called listening to the wild wisdom of the forest, to the realms of the divine feminine with its earthed-body nature knowledge. But then, as these stories often remind us, there is an important task – to bring this knowledge back from the forest to the 'village'. Significant questions are: 'Who are these words in service of?', 'How do we bring this wisdom and these new words back to an existing culture of living and of practice?'

This has often been turned into a simple issue of translation, changing forest words back into the traditional forms and words of pre-existing cultural, academic convention, for example. However, I think that this considerably dilutes the impact of the wisdom, for form is a major part of the message. It has been my experience that, once people connect somatically with the earth, the artistic realm – music, movement, poetry, sculpture – is the medium of communication. These gifted forms arising from the land offer us new conceptualizations, new terminology and, importantly, a channel to find the necessary humility to move into the right relationship with this beautiful planet.

Hence, I offer my poem first; this is my first and true

response, from the sky–earth axis. A gift to David and Keith … from here.

> Finally, I offer my name …
> The earth tells me I am an earthsoul dreamer.
> I tell the human 'world' I am an ecological practitioner.

A possibility of wholeness to relish

Rebecca Freeth

Reading David and Keith's words, the message I hear most insistently is a warning about centrality and appropriation. Their metatheory offers a clear line to avoid falling heedlessly into these traps.

I am a white woman, living and working in South Africa as a social change facilitator. I specialize in facilitating collaboration across deep divides. Although ecotherapy is not my field, I recognize David and Keith's warning.

As a facilitator, I graduated from working in dingy church halls to soulless hotel venues. When I could not bear it anymore, I started to gravitate outdoors. I was delighted to take groups into the fresh air, to walk among the trees and to have the sounds of birds and rivers accompany our solo times and dialogues. Then one day, while teaching a course on facilitation – where we moved between the classroom and the abundant untamed gardens outside – a student spoke most cogently about 'nature as the facilitator'. I remember being pulled up short by this idea. Surely a bridge too far. I am the facilitator. Nature offers a wonderful setting for groups, but it is my preparation, skill and presence that facilitate the group process. Otherwise, what am I doing there?

As a white person, I have sat in countless conversation circles with South Africans of diverse racial identities. Sometimes I am facilitating; sometimes I am participating. Sometimes nature is the facilitator. These conversations have gone to depths I could never have imagined. I have found myself learning at a breath-taking speed as the conversation unfolds. Exhilarated, trying out new ideas as I speak them. In those moments, I feel deeply connected. I belong. On one of these occasions, I remember a Black woman speaking up from the edge of the group, 'Why can't you white people see how central you are?' I woke as if from a reverie of joyful ease to the fact, that as white people, we had taken over the conversation, failing to notice in our exuberance the effect this was having on the rest of the group.

When I am caught up in this centrality buzz, it is surprisingly easy to take up more than my share of space and voice, and to appropriate things that are not mine. To recycle ideas that I heard elsewhere and to take credit for them as mine, to believe that they are mine. I get it now when I hear Black colleagues say: 'I share an idea in groups and it doesn't go anywhere. Then a white person says what I just said and the group gets excited about it.'

When I look deeper into these experiences, I find that the comfort and ease of centrality – whether as a facilitator or as a white person – can also have a cocooning effect. To be at the centre is also to be protected and insulated, whereas being at the margins is to be more exposed, including to harsh realities. While I stay cocooned in the centre, I risk becoming less relevant and less able to navigate those harsh realities. My perception narrows. More than that, my humanity narrows. If there is some truth in that, then the question returns: What am I doing here? Am I helping or am I getting in the way?

Keith and Dave write that 'if the therapist, as the one curating the therapy, privileges themselves over any other source of relationship, then they effectively *get in the way* of the therapeutic process' (my emphasis).

Then I come face to face with the possibility of being redundant and irrelevant in the world I occupy. And I find myself musing whether one of the drivers of rampaging colonial appropriation was a deeply unconscious fear of being irrelevant and redundant. An unprocessed idea and one worth further exploration, but not in these pages.

The antidote to centrality and appropriation does not lie in heroic helpfulness. I tried that and it did not work. Some years ago, I was involved in an initiative designed to re-ignite the conversation about post-colonial and post-apartheid restitution, after centuries of racist appropriation. Political power had been redistributed, but economic power had not; a tiny minority of white South Africans still owned the vast majority of the country's land, industry and capital. We nicknamed ourselves the 'white accountability' initiative and were just beginning to build up a head of steam when we asked for a conversation with a group of Black friends and colleagues, to hear whether this initiative made sense to them. It did not.

> Jonas said: 'If you give, you bring your demons. Your giving has cost us Black people so much. Stop giving. There isn't an answer. There's no goal to reach.'
>
> Loyiso wept as he listened and then told us: 'You have to heal first. White people need to heal white people. You need to find your own beauty and wholeness. You don't know your own worth.'

It has taken a long time to soak up the full import of this response and to turn towards this kind of healing. Combining what Jonas and Loyiso told us with David and Keith's metatheory helps to express a possibility I can relish. It is this: believing that I am nature (reciprocal paradigm) and that nature heals (ecocentric paradigm) relieves someone like me of the need to be central and helpful. That does not imply being irrelevant or redundant, but instead offers the freedom to belong as just another 'plain member' of the ecosphere (Leopold, 1949, as cited by Dave and Keith in Chapter 4), modestly bringing my nature-endowed beauty and worth, burdened by neither a need to appropriate nor a need to compensate, but rather, to seek wholeness within and in relationship. And to do so without performing feats of spiritual bypassing that gloss over the devastating legacies of white supremacy. Luckily, the authors do not claim that it is simple to navigate the line of ecological contradiction.

From theory to practice: reflections from the field

Rupert Hutchinson

What does it mean to conduct our work ecocentrically and reciprocally as outdoor practitioners and therapists? How might we not only understand the theoretical and philosophical foundations of the field, but truly embody the values that underpin the ecotherapeutic modality, in service of those we work with, as well as all living systems we depend on?

The following reflection is based on over fifteen years of working with a broad range of people outdoors, often in remote parts of the world, for extended periods of time – from adventure travel and outdoor instruction, to bespoke personal development and sustainability leadership programmes.

I am an outdoor guide; I am not a therapist. However, throughout all of my work I have seen richness, depth and profound meaning come from outdoor experiences that I would describe as therapeutic. The experiences I refer to here all share a common thread which I have witnessed time and again, in a multitude of different ways: when individuals experience a felt sense of being part of something much larger. This often leads to radical shifts in perspective on self and the ways in which we are in relationship with the world around us. They lie beyond the growing evidence base of proven health and wellbeing benefits of being outdoors, or the sense of reward that can come from meeting the aims and goals often associated with outdoor activities.

Although hard to articulate, especially as these experiences are so deeply personal, it seems clear as a practitioner that they can momentarily bring us into a state where the bounds of the individual self expand out into a wider sense of self, inextricably connected to, and an inherent part of, everything else. I have experienced this often myself and witnessed it many times in others – even just for the briefest of moments – and it can be profoundly transformative, especially when processed and integrated in a structured way.

My belief is that this is a felt, rather than a cognitive, experience of our ecological reality, and one that is always available to us, but for many reasons in our modern world it can be challenging to access. However, I have come to see the intention to help facilitate these experiences as the primary focus of my work and a key part of the responsibility I have as an outdoor practitioner. This is mostly due to my conviction that experiences of this felt sense of a wider self act as a catalyst for genuine shifts in pro-ecological behaviour towards creating a more just and regenerative world.

A vital question that emerges from this book therefore is this: what does it require of me, as an outdoor practitioner, to operate in a genuinely reciprocal and ecocentric way? I believe that at least part of the answer is both radical and counter-cultural – challenging traditional roles and cultural norms, and inviting us to hold both the practical and the intangible with equal regard.

For me to operate reciprocally as a facilitator, with the worldview of 'human as nature', I have to absolutely embody it – not only theoretically understand what it means but truly feel it.

That feeling is something that can, and should as a practitioner, be cultivated. It should lie as a foundation of any ecotherapeutic engagement – particularly as this is the very feeling I am hoping to help catalyse in others.

What that looks like will be different for everyone, but for me it involves the continuing practice of attuning and (re)sensitizing my physiological and psychological faculties to the world around me, through curiosity, observation and spending significant time, often alone, in outdoor spaces, particularly ones where human systems are less dominant.

For me to operate ecocentrically, with 'nature as therapist', I have to learn how to balance the task of both structure and fluidity, acknowledging that paradoxically I have an important role to play, but, really, it is not about me at all.

If the aim is to help increase the potential for people to experience the ecological self, then all I can do is help facilitate the process, to seek to create the conditions that make it as easy as possible to occur. Theory, tools, methods and an understanding of when to deploy them are vital, but there's also the need to be open and aware of the surroundings, and the richness of particular and unique emergent moments and dynamic events that are constantly revealing themselves when outdoors – moments where the potential for a sense of connection to something bigger or broader is heightened.

In drawing attention to a subtle moment of stillness on a mountain top, or the drama and tension of an approaching storm, the complexity of an ant hill, the trembling of aspen leaves in the breeze. Once trust and rapport have been cultivated with a group, and a safe container has been created, taking time to invite people to pause, become present and engage during these moments, often also integrating simple acts of secular ritual into the process, can be powerful and meaningful.

As a facilitator I am constantly aiming to be open and aware of what is presenting itself, and what is calling my attention, in myself, the group or the surroundings. Intuition and the ability to navigate emergence are key. This, for me, is a subtle combination of experience and awareness – there have been countless times where an intuitive 'hunch' has led to something extraordinary.

The balance lies in being able, confident and willing to follow these hunches, to offer people an invitation, then step away, allowing the richness of the moment to take hold (or not! There are no guarantees of course – people's experiences naturally depend on their individual capacity and willingness to engage). Over time, experience has shown me that, as soon as 'I' get in the way too much, the process is liable to be derailed, trying to programme in a 'transformative experience', getting caught up in fixed goals and outcomes, or allowing my own insecurities to creep in.

I have therefore found it a necessity as an outdoor practitioner to align myself with ecocentric values and to cultivate ongoing and in-depth self-reflection and enquiry – via coaching, supervision, therapy or otherwise – to be able to identify my patterns, or parts, that might get in the way of allowing nature to act as therapist.

To work reciprocally and ecocentrically is complex, nuanced and calls us to operate in ways that require not only theoretical and philosophical understanding, but extensive experience in the field, continual development of our own felt experience of 'human as nature' and the personal work required to cultivate self-awareness and intuition.

I do not believe it is necessarily imperative to be a qualified therapist to facilitate ethical and potentially transformative experiences outdoors, especially as the focus, as I see it, is on the felt experience of our interrelatedness to the rest of nature, not on the processing of specific personal and human challenges. This is a different approach to practising psychotherapy outdoors, where the focus is more on the modality and client relationship, with nature acting as a 'therapy room'.

I do believe, however, that to work ethically and safely in any leadership capacity outdoors requires a base level of training, skill and understanding appropriate to the landscape, whether a local forest or a remote mountain side. Training in navigation, group management, appropriate clothing and equipment, emergency procedures and first aid should all come first. These are fundamental outdoor leadership responsibilities. The subtleties of facilitation mentioned above grow out of this practical foundation which helps to create the safe container needed for meaningful experiences to occur.

This is an emergent field, and there's much work to be done in terms of defining best practices and ways of working. There is a growing need for training opportunities that speak to the essential practical skills, extensive personal practice and nuanced facilitation required to operate in this field in a way that is aligned with reciprocal and ecocentric values.

Lastly, perhaps the most challenging to articulate, is the

inherent ambiguity and mystery in all of this. As a human I am not sure I can really know exactly what is going on when we spend intentional and quality time in wild places – what it stirs in us and what that all means. Perhaps all we will ever be in a position to do is to safely and gently hold spaces for ourselves and the people we work with to engage with that wider sense of self that is always there, always inviting us into the extraordinariness of life on this beautiful planet we call home, and calling us to action in whatever form that takes.

Reflections

David Key and Keith Tudor

Although written independently and from diverse contexts, the responses in this chapter share many common stories. Some align with those explored in the preceding text, whereas others deepen and extend the dialogue, calling for whatever might come next and inviting further conversation. So, here, we offer our reflections on these responses.

We hear stories about language – Badimaya/Badimia, Māori, Bundjalung and Samoan, as well as English. We hear about the challenge to English as the assumed norm by which to name and in which to understand the world: land, Country, wind, bird song, hum, rustle, spirits, crow, breeze, moana … and of people talking with ancestors and beings in trees. We hear stories about where language should come from, how it should emerge, from the 'ground-human-up, not the human-top-down'. We also hear that, at times, where the white person repeats the story, all is suddenly heard – while others are silenced.

We hear stories about words and, specifically, words that are different to those used in Western science: waiting, sensing, connecting, breathing with, receiving – before responding. We hear the recognition of 'the cry in these pages', both in the tears of loss and grief, and in the call to action. We read about different practices and different arguments and emphases, each contribution bringing a pause, a juxtaposition, a challenge and a new knowing: at least 'we now know all the words that [ecotherapy] is not!' These words and phrases, as well as the space between them, highlight their own woeful inadequacy for describing the subject, the crises we face and the powerful healing experiences that form ecotherapy's green heart.

We hear stories of poetry and the different rhythm and drum beat of their universes. We love the way in which the poetry illustrates, synthesizes, distils, intensifies, stretches and challenges the ideas, writing and theory contained in the previous chapters. We hear a call to listen, beyond the human voice and beyond the dominance of reason, rationale and intellect, especially as expressed in the Western tradition, and to listen to 'the words that arise from the earthed-body'. The ancient lineage woven through First Nations of what some now refer to as ecotherapy is brought into sharp focus: 'we have always healed this way.' There is a common call for sensory, somatic, direct contact with the rest of nature to be at the heart of any ecotherapy practice: 'this is a felt, rather than cognitive, experience of our ecological reality'.

We hear stories of spirit, of 'the felt sense of being part of something much larger', of the 'honouring of ancestors and spirit', of the 'surrender to reciprocal flow'. We are told that from a First Nations' perspective ecotherapy is a 'simplified, two-dimensional concept', clumsily trying to describe something vast and mysterious that includes 'a space that is non-linear, timeless, physical and spiritual'. From other perspectives, it feels like spirit is felt and deeply desired, striven for, craved even. How to embrace it through ecotherapy, however, is still unclear, obscured by Western forms, shallow New Ageism, self-doubt and the pejoratives of mass media and popular culture. The sacralization of nature through ecotherapy offers redemption, 'the freedom to belong'. It offers to bring diverse human communities together, including those most responsible for past and present ecological destruction, into relationship with the planet as a whole. But to those of us who depend on our industrial growth culture, and its dis-ease, for their livelihoods, a spiritual ecotherapy also offers potential destitution. Plagued by insecurities about validity, credibility, professional status and isolation, many would-be ecotherapists fearfully retreat from matters of spirit. This is perhaps the field's greatest challenge, far beyond finding philosophical congruence or a common language.

We hear stories of place: of Country, of sea, of diaspora, of Lightwood, of Africa – and of the wounding and 'the pain of place', and being misplaced and displaced.

We hear critical stories – of ecopsychology as forgetting spirit and ignoring ancestors. Of colonization and re-colonization. Of past trauma and new trauma ... of division and othering ... At every step, the responses expose dualisms. The metatheory holds a strange position in this regard. It is itself divided either side of an ecological line, creating yet another dualism. And yet one side of the line is non-dual, revealing the deep paradox of dualism itself – that it coexists with non-dualism and that each depends entirely on the other.

We hear stories of challenge – to honour, specifically, Indigenous medicine and ancestors; of naming; of acknowledgement and recognition; of seeing, of not seeing, and of not being seen – and by the generosity of colleagues not only taking up our invitation to contribute but also extending that invitation to others, beyond, to enter this yarn, kōrero, conversation, dialogue. There is a challenge to shift the place of humans generally, and ecotherapists specifically, away from the centre of nature and from the centre of the therapeutic process. Sometimes this is into a role learnt through millennia of ecocentric ritual and ancient practice. Other times this loss of centrality opens to bewilderment and a desire for forms as yet unknown within industrial growth cultures. Either way, it is clear that the anthropocentric therapist must be challenged; they must yield to an altogether more humble and wildly relational role.

We hear stories of connection, of opening to our senses and feelings and of trusting our intuition and creativity: stories of breath, body, animal, ocean, sky and of wildness. We hear stories of reinhabiting our earthy selves.

We hear stories of practice. Among the wrestling with words, paradoxes and contradictions are calls for professional practice to meet various conditions, extending beyond the narrative of our book toward something less theoretical and altogether more pragmatic. Of these, there are two conditions that stand out. The first, and most important, is that ecotherapists themselves must maintain ongoing personal practices to help keep them – in an embodied, intuitive and spiritual way – feeling connected to the rest of nature. The second is that the practice of ecotherapy, as it is presented here at least, must take place outside, under the sky. For these conditions to be met safely, ethically and effectively, a third condition must be met. Ecotherapists must know how to lead themselves and others outdoors, safely and effectively – at the very least to meet the physical demands of the places in which they intend to work. This last point is a duty of care. Achieving this practical competence, of course, can be done in myriad ways that are place based, culturally appropriate and that honour diversity.

These are the stories we hear.

Thank you for your stories.

6.

Conclusion

There are numerous overlapping and ambiguous terms used to describe approaches and practices within the emerging field of ecotherapy, some of which have meanings that are contradictory, counterproductive and even divisive. Other terms bring cohesion, community and positive change.

Although many definitions and practices remain impossible to categorize meaningfully as a single word, term or phase, they can be better understood by tracing their history and development – and, as this book advocates, exploring and characterizing the philosophical perspectives they represent. Even so, there are many vagaries that remain unresolved, though perhaps this is entirely appropriate in an emergent new field – one that encompasses the wild, the chaotic and the messy. Nevertheless, as all practice is founded on theory, and all theory is unpinned by philosophy, it is important for practitioners to know their theory and the ground on which they are standing – a point that seems particularly pertinent for ecotherapists.

As with law, ignorance of theory, philosophy and context is no excuse. There is, as we note, the danger that some terms and practices used in the field of ecotherapy are culturally insensitive and appropriative and, in some cases, cause personal and cultural re-traumatization (Jones & Segal, 2018). In this context, we encourage practitioners to think carefully about the way we describe our work, the meaning of those descriptions and how we support or undermine practice, however unwittingly. Another philosophical and political danger is that ecopsychology and ecotherapy become co-opted into the cultural paradigms that they are trying to challenge and change, for example, where nature is used as a therapeutic resource, thus replicating the consumer culture that has damaged it so devastatingly, or where ecopsychology and ecotherapy become regulated and controlled by the same institutions that promote individualism, thereby denying our essential ecology. This could happen almost by accident, simply through a lack of diligent, critical awareness.

In response to these considerations and dangers, we offer not only this scoping review of the field of ecotherapy but also a metatheory and paradigms that we find particularly useful, both as an organizing idea and as providing philosophical congruence for theory and practice. We hope that they help ecotherapy practitioners to ensure that their practice is more aligned with their philosophy, both implicitly and explicitly. At the very least, we think that great care should be taken by ecotherapists in how we practise and describe our work, as many of the terms currently being used are culturally inappropriate and therapeutically counterproductive.

While offering a metatheory, we are acutely aware that maps, specific terms, theories and models evolve, and we share Rogers' (1959) perspective that 'theory … is – a fallible, changing attempt to construct a network of gossamer threads which will contain the solid facts … [but only] as a stimulus to further creative thinking' (p. 191). Also, differences are going to emerge through any attempt at categorization, which, as Foucault (1966) points out, are always arbitrary and culturally embedded. As with all language, semantics highlight differences which then create discourse, and conflict. On the other hand, semantics can also unearth similitude and, stepping back to a wider frame of perspective, can allow a deepening and widening of awareness and connection. It is in this spirit that we offer 'a', not 'the', ecotherapy field guide.

This book is not about the day-to-day practice of ecotherapy, beyond calling for it to be consciously connected to philosophical, and ultimately literal, ground. It is crystal clear from the responses to our work here, that, although it is necessary and helpful to make this call, and to invite a deeper dialogue about the nomenclature and framing of this evolving field, the real hunger is for practice: real, somatic, visceral, earthy, direct, creative, wild and unmediated practice.

Our final call is for us all to seek ways to bring together contemporary forms of practice that honour history, support diversity and remain true to the ecological ground of ecotherapy. Human beings can only ever be healed as part of the planet upon which we depend. Anything less is temporary and fatal.

REFERENCES

Note: the access dates for all websites have been checked and verified and are correct at the time of going to press.

Abram, D. (1996). *The Spell of the Sensuous: Perception and Language in a More-than-Human World*. Random House.

Adorno, T. W. (1951). *Minima Moralia: Reflections From a Damaged Life* (E. F. N. Jephcott, trans.). Verso (reprinted 1978).

Adorno, T. W. & Horkheimer, M. (1947). *Dialectic of Enlightenment* (E. F. N. Jephcott, trans.). Stanford University Press (reprinted 2002).

Al-Krenawi, A. (1999). An overview of rituals in Western therapies and intervention: Argument for their use in cross-cultural therapy. *International Journal for the Advancement of Counselling*, 21: 3–17. https://doi.org/10.1023/A:1005311925402.

Allison, K. W., Crawford, I., Echemendia, R., Robinson, L. & Knepp, D. (1994). Human diversity and professional competence: Training in clinical and counseling psychology revisited. *American Psychologist*, 49: 792–796. https://doi.org/10.1037/0003-066X.49.9.792.

Andrews, K. (1999). The wilderness expedition as a rite of passage: Meaning and process in experiential education. *Journal of Experiential Education*, 22: 35–43. https://doi.org/10.1177/105382599902200107.

Anthony, C. (1995). Ecopsychology and the deconstruction of whiteness. In: T. E. Roszak, M. E. Gomes & A. D. Kanner (Eds.), *Ecopsychology: Restoring the Earth, Healing the Mind* (pp. 263–278). Sierra Club Books.

Anzieu, D. (1989). *The Skin Ego*. Yale University Press.

Applebaum, B. (2016). Critical whiteness studies. *Oxford Research Encyclopaedia of Education*. https://doi.org/10.1093/acrefore/9780190264093.013.5.

Arksey, H. & O'Malley, L. (2005). Scoping studies: Towards a methodological framework. *International Journal of Social Research Methodology*, 8: 19–32. https://doi.org/10.1080/1364557032000119616.

Armstrong, J. (1995). Keepers of the earth. In: T. E. Roszak, M. E. Gomes & A. D. Kanner (Eds.), *Ecopsychology: Restoring the Earth, Healing the Mind* (pp. 316–24). Sierra Club Books.

Bacon, S. B. & Kimball, R. (1989). The wilderness challenge model. In: R.D. Lyman, S. Prentice-Dunn & S. Gabel (Eds.), *Residential and Inpatient Treatment of Children and Adolescents* (pp. 115–144). Springer.

Bateson, N. (2016). *Small Arcs of Larger Circles: Framing through Other Patterns*. Triarchy Press.

Beels, C. C. (2007). Psychotherapy as a rite of passage. *Family Process*, 46: 421–436. https://doi.org/10.1111/j.1545-5300.2007.00223.x.

Berger, R. (2004). Therapeutic aspects of nature therapy. *Therapy through the Arts – The Journal of the Israeli Association of Creative and Expressive Therapies*, 3: 60–69.

Berger, R. (2008). Nature therapy: Developing a framework for practice. Unpublished doctoral thesis, University of Abertay. https://rke.abertay.ac.uk/ws/portalfiles/portal/15733398/Berger_2009_Nature_therapy_developing_a_framework_PhD.pdf.

Berger, R. & McLeod, J. (2006). Incorporating nature into therapy: A framework for practice. *Journal of Systemic Therapies*, 25(2): 80–94. https://doi.org/10.1521/jsyt.2006.25.2.80.

Berger, R. & Tiry, M. (2012). The enchanting forest and the healing sand – Nature therapy with people coping with psychiatric difficulties. *The Arts in Psychotherapy*, 39: 412–416. https://doi.org/10.1016/j.aip.2012.03.009.

Bernal, M. E. & Castro, F. G. (1994). Are clinical psychologists prepared for service and research with ethnic minorities? Report of a decade of progress. *American Psychologist*, 49: 797–805. https://doi.org/10.1037/0003-066X.49.9.797.

Berne, E. (1961). *Transactional Analysis Psychotherapy: A Systematic Individual and Social Psychiatry*. Grove Press.

Bhabha, H. (1994). *The Location of Culture*. Routledge.

Bloom, K., Galanter, M. & Reeve, S. (2014). *Embodied Lives: Reflections on the Influence of Suprapto Suryodarmo and Amerta Movement*. Triarchy Press.

Britton, E., Kindermann, G., Domegan, C. & Carlin, C. (2018). Blue care: A systematic review of blue space interventions for health and wellbeing. *Health Promotion International*, 35: 50–69. https://doi.org/10.1093/heapro/day103.

Buckley, R. (2020). Nature tourism and mental health: Parks, happiness, and causation. *Journal of Sustainable Tourism*, 28: 1409–1424. https://doi.org/10.1080/09669582.2020.1742725.

Burns, G. W. (1998). *Nature-Guided Therapy: Brief Integrative Strategies for Health and Well-Being*. Routledge.

Buzzell, L. (2016). The many ecotherapies. In: M. Jordan & J. Hinds (Eds.), *Ecotherapy: Theory, Research & Practice* (pp. 70–82). Palgrave Macmillan.

Buzzell, L. & Chalquist, C., Eds. (2009). *Ecotherapy: Healing with Nature in Mind*. Counterpoint Press.

Carson, R. L. (1965). *Silent Spring*. Penguin.

Caulkins, M. C., White, D. D. & Russell, K. C. (2006). The role of physical exercise in wilderness therapy for troubled adolescent women. *Journal of Experiential Education*, 29: 18–37. https://doi.org/10.1177/105382590602900104.

Chalquist, C. (2007). *What Is Terrapsychology?* www.chalquist.com/terrapsychologydefined.

Chalquist, C. (2011). *Ventral Depths: Alchemical Themes and Mythic Motifs of the Great Central Valley of California*. World Soul Press.

Chalquist, C. (2020). *Terrapsychological Inquiry: Restorying Our Relationship with Nature, Place, and Planet*. Routledge.

Clayton, S. & Myers, G. (2009). *Conservation Psychology: Understanding and Promoting Human Care for Nature*. Wiley-Blackwell.

Clinebell, H. (1996). *Ecotherapy: Healing Ourselves, Healing the Earth*. Routledge.

Coleman, M. (2010). *Awake in the Wild: Mindfulness in Nature as a Path of Self-Discovery*. New World Library.

Conn, L. K. & Conn, S. A. (2009). Opening to the other. In: L. Buzzell & C. Chalquist (Eds.), *Ecotherapy: Healing with Nature in Mind* (pp. 111–115). Counterpoint Press.

Conn, S. A. (1990). Protest and thrive: The relationship between global responsibility and personal empowerment. *New England Journal of Public Policy*, 6: 163–177. https://scholarworks.umb.edu/nejpp/vol6/iss1/18.

Conn, S. A. (1992). *From Information to Transformation*. Center for Psychology and Social Change Forum, 29 September 1992.

Coote, A., Allen, J. & Woodhead, D. (2004). *Finding Out What Works. Building Knowledge about Complex, Community-Based Initiatives*. King's Fund.

Crisp, S. (1998). *International Models of Best Practice in Wilderness and*

Adventure Therapy. https://files.eric.ed.gov/fulltext/ED424052.pdf

Danziger, K. (2006). Universalism and indigenization in the history of modern psychology. In: A. C. Brock (ed), *Internationalizing the History of Psychology* (pp. 208–225). University Press.

Davis, J. V. (2011). Ecopsychology, transpersonal psychology, and nonduality. *International Journal of Transpersonal Studies*, 30: 137–147. https://doi.org/10.1002/9781118591277.ch33.

DeMayo, N. (2009). Horses, humans and healing. In: L. Buzzell & C. Chalquist (Eds.), *Ecotherapy: Healing with Nature in Mind* (pp. 149–156). Counterpoint Press.

Dewey, J. (1938). Experience and education. *The Educational Forum*, 50: 241–252. https://doi.org/10.1080/00131728609335764.

Diehm, C. (2006). Arne Næss and the task of Gestalt ontology. *Environmental Ethics*, 28: 21–35. www.pdcnet.org/enviroethics/content/enviroethics_2006_0028_0001_0021_0035.

Doherty, T. J. (2009). A peer-reviewed journal for ecopsychology. *Ecopsychology*, 1, 1–7. https://doi.org/10.1089/eco.2009.0101.edi.

Ducarme, F. & Couvet, D. (2020). What does 'nature' mean? *Palgrave Communications*, 6: 14. www.nature.com/articles/s41599-020-0390-y.

Elwy, A. R., Groessl, E. J., Eisen, S. V., Riley, K. E., Maiya, M., Lee, J. P., Sarkin, A. & Park, C. L. (2014). A systematic scoping review of yoga intervention components and study quality. *American Journal of Preventive Medicine*, 47: 220–232. https://doi.org/10.1016/j.amepre.2014.03.012.

Enari, D. & Viliamu Jameson, L. (2021). Climate justice: A Pacific Island perspective. *Australian Journal of Human Rights*, 27: 149–160. https://doi.org/10.1080/1323238X.2021.1950905.

Fanon, F. (1961). *The Wretched of the Earth* (C. Farrington, Trans.). Grove Press (reprinted 1963).

Fisher, A. (2013a). *Radical Ecopsychology: Psychology in Service to Life*, 2nd edn. SUNY Press.

Fisher, A. (2013b). Ecopsychology at the crossroads: Contesting the nature of a field. *Ecopsychology*, 5: 167–176. https://doi.org/10.1089/eco.2013.0031.

Fisher, A. (2016). Going deep: A review of *Environmental Melancholia: Psychoanalytic Dimensions of Engagement by Renee Lertzman. Ecopsychology*, 8: 222–227. https://doi.org/10.1089/eco.2016.0021

Fisher, A. (2019). Ecopsychology as decolonial praxis. *Ecopsychology*, 11: 145–155. https://doi.org/10.1089/eco.2019.0008.

Foucault, M. (1966). *Les Mots et les Choses* [Words and Things]. Éditions Gallimard.

Fox, W. (1992). Intellectual origins of the 'depth' theme in the philosophy of Arne Naess. *The Trumpeter: Journal of Ecosophy*, 9, 68–73. https://trumpeter.athabascau.ca/index.php/trumpet/article/view/427/699.

Furuyashiki, A., Tabuchi, K., Norikoshi, K., Kobayashi, T. & Oriyama, S. (2019). A comparative study of the physiological and psychological effects of forest bathing (Shinrin-yoku) on working age people with and without depressive tendencies. *Environmental Health and Preventive Medicine*, 24: 46. https://doi.org/10.1186/s12199-019-0800-1.

Gass, M. A. (1993). *Adventure Therapy: Therapeutic Applications of Adventure Programming*. Association for Experiential Education and Kendall/Hunt.

Giroux, H. (1997). Rewriting the discourse of racial identity: Towards a pedagogy and politics of whiteness. *Harvard Educational Review*, 67: 285–321. https://doi.org/10.17763/haer.67.2.r4523gh4176677u8.

Glendinning, C. (1995). Technology, trauma and the wild. In: T. E. Roszak, M. E. Gomes, & A. D. Kanner (Eds.), *Ecopsychology: Restoring the Earth, Healing the Mind* (pp. 41–54). Sierra Club Books.

Global Indigenous Data Alliance. (2019). *CARE Principles for Indigenous Data Governance*. www.gida-global.org/care.

Gomes, M. & Kanner, A. (1995). The rape of the well maidens: Feminist psychology and the environmental crisis. In: T. E. Roszak, M. E. Gomes & A. D. Kanner (Eds.), *Ecopsychology: Restoring the Earth, Healing the Mind* (pp. 111–121). Sierra Club Books.

Gone, J. P. (2008). Mental health discourse as Western cultural proselytization. *ETHOS*, 36: 310–315. https://doi.org/10.1111/j.1548-1352.2008.00016.x.

Gone, J. P. (2010). Psychotherapy and traditional healing for American Indians: Exploring the prospects for therapeutic integration. *The Counseling Psychologist*, 38: 166–235. https://doi.org/10.1177/0011000008330831.

Gone, J. P. & Kirmayer, L. J. (2020). Advancing Indigenous mental health research: Ethical, conceptual and methodological challenges. *Transcultural Psychiatry*, 57: 235–249. https://doi.org/10.1177/1363461520923151.

Gullone, E. (2000). The biophilia hypothesis and life in the 21st century: Increasing mental health or increasing pathology? *Journal of Happiness Studies*, 1: 293–322. https://doi.org/10.1023/A:1010043827986.

Häber, M. R. (2020). Unattended trauma of the San Lorenzo River: A terrapsychological inquiry. Doctoral dissertation, California Institute of Integral Studies. www.proquest.com/openview/f99003e532c251140255e1543bb5ec07/1.

Haeckel, E. H. P. A. (1876). *The History of Creation: Or the Development of the Earth and Its Inhabitants by the Action of Natural Causes* (E. R. Lankester, Trans). H. S. King & Son.

Hansen, M. M., Jones, R. & Tocchini, K. (2017). Shinrin-yoku (forest bathing) and nature therapy: A state-of-the-art review. *International Journal of Environmental Research and Public Health*, 14: 851. https://doi.org/10.3390/ijerph14080851.

Hasbach, P. H. (2012). Ecotherapy. In: P. H. Kahn & P. H. Hasbach (Eds.), *Ecopsychology: Science, Totems, and the Technological Species* (pp. 115–140). MIT Press.

Hassink, J. & Van Dijk, M., Eds. (2006). *Farming for Health: Green-Care Farming across Europe and the United States of America*. Springer.

Haughey, M. (2016). Widening our lens – Towards a new model of psychotherapy [Paper presentation]. In: A. Kilcoyne (ed), *Book of Presentations and Workshops from the 2016 IAHIP Conference* (p. 134–139). Irish Association of Humanistic and Integrative Psychotherapy.

Hau'ofa, E. (2008). *We are the Ocean: Selected Works*. University of Hawai'i Press.

Hayes, K., Blashki, G., Wiseman, J., Burke, S. & Reifels, L. (2018). Climate change and mental health: Risks, impacts and priority actions. *International Journal of Mental Health Systems*, 12: 1–12. https://doi.org/10.1186/s13033-018-0210-6.

Heidegger, M. (1977). *The Question Concerning Technology and Other Essays*. Garland.

Hill, N. (2007). Wilderness therapy as a treatment modality for at-risk youth: A primer for mental health counselors. *Journal of Mental Health Counseling*, 29: 338–349. https://doi.org/10.17744/mehc.29.4.c6121j162j143178.

Ho, D. Y. (1998). Indigenous psychologies: Asian perspectives. *Journal of Cross-Cultural Psychology*, 29: 88–103. https://doi.org/10.1177/0022022198291005.

Ibes, D., Hirama, I. & Schuyler, C. (2018). Greenspace ecotherapy interventions: The stress-reduction potential of green micro-breaks integrating nature connection and mind-body skills. *Ecopsychology*, 10: 137–150. https://doi.org/10.1089/eco.2018.0024.

Ideno, Y., Hayashi, K., Abe, Y., Ueda, K., Iso, H., Noda, M., Lee, J.-S. & Suzuki, S. (2017). Blood pressure-lowering effect of Shinrin-yoku (Forest bathing): A systematic review and meta-analysis. *BMC Complementary and Alternative Medicine*, 17: 409. https://doi.org/10.1186/s12906-017-1912-z.

Intergovernmental Panel on Climate Change (2018). Summary for policymakers. In: V. Masson-Delmotte, P. Zhai, H. -O. Pörtner, D. Roberts, J. Skea, P. R. Shukla, A. Pirani, W. Moufouma-Okia, C. Péan, R. Pidcock, S. Connors, J. B. R. Matthews, Y. Chen, X. Zhou, M. I. Gomis, E. Lonnoy, T. Maycock, M. Tignor & T. Waterfield (Eds.), *IPCC Special Report Global Warming of 1.5°C*. World Meteorological Organization.

Jahoda, G. (2016). On the rise and decline of 'Indigenous psychology'. *Culture & Psychology*, 22: 169–181. https://doi.org/10.1177/1354067X16634052.

Jones, A. T. & Segal, D. S. (2018). Unsettling ecopsychology: Addressing settler colonialism in ecopsychology practice. *Ecopsychology*, 10: 127–136. https://doi.org/10.1089/eco.2018.0059

Jordan, M. (2016). Ecotherapy as psychotherapy: Towards an ecopsychotherapy. In: M. Jordan & J. Hinds (Eds.), *Ecotherapy: Theory, Research and Practice* (pp. 58–69). Palgrave Macmillan.

Jung, C. G., ed (1968). *Man and His Symbols*. Random House.

Jung, C. G. (1989). *Memories, Dreams, Reflections* (C. Winston & R. Winston, trans., A. Jaffe, ed, revised edn). Vintage.

Jung, W. H., Woo, J. M., & Ryu J. S. (2015). Effect of a forest therapy program and the forest environment on female workers' stress. *Urban Forestry & Urban Greening*, 14: 274–281. https://doi.org/10.1016/j.ufug.2015.02.004.

Kahn, P. H. & Hasbach, P. H., Eds. (2012). *Ecopsychology: Science, Totems, and the Technological Species*. MIT Press.

Kanner, A. & Gomes, M. (1995). The all-consuming self. In: T. E. Roszak, M. E. Gomes & A. D. Kanner (Eds.), *Ecopsychology: Restoring the Earth, Healing the Mind* (pp. 77–91). Sierra Club Books.

Kamioka, H., Tsutani, K., Mutoh, Y., Honda, T., Shiozawa, N., Okada, S., Park, S., Kitayuguchi, J., Kamada, M., Okuizumi, H. & Handa, S. (2012). A systematic review of randomized controlled trials on curative and health enhancement effects of forest therapy. *Psychology Research and Behavior Management*, 5: 85–95. https://doi.org/10.2147/PRBM.S32402.

Kaplan S. & Talbot J. F. (1983). Psychological benefits of a wilderness experience. In: I. Altman & J. F. Wohlwill (Eds.), *Behavior and the Natural Environment* (pp. 163–203). Springer.

Kellert, S. R. & Wilson, E. O. (1993). *The Biophilia Hypothesis*. Island Press.

Kerr, M. & Key, D. (2012). The ecology of the unconscious. In: M. J. Rust & N. Totton (Eds.), *Vital Signs: Psychological Responses to Ecological Crisis* (pp. 63–78). Karnac.

Khalsa, S. B. S. (2013). Yoga for psychiatry and mental health: An ancient practice with modern relevance. *Indian Journal of Psychiatry*, 55: S334–36. www.ncbi.nlm.nih.gov/pmc/articles/PMC3768207.

Kidner, D. (2001). *Nature and Psyche: Radical Environmentalism and the Politics of Subjectivity*. SUNY Press.

Kim, K. J., Wee, S. J., Gilbert, B. B. & Choi, J. (2016). Young children's physical and psychological well-being through yoga. *Childhood Education*, 92: 437–445. https://doi.org/10.1080/00094056.2016.1251792.

Kim, U. & Berry, J. W. (Eds.) (1993). *Indigenous Psychologies: Research and Experience in Cultural Context*. Sage Publications.

Kirmayer, L. J. (2007). Psychotherapy and the cultural concept of the person. *Transcultural Psychiatry*, 44: 232–257. https://doi.org/10.1177/1363461506070794.

Kohak, E. (1984). *The Embers and the Stars: Philosophical Inquiry into the Moral Sense of Nature*. University of Chicago Press.

Kolb, D. A. (2014). *Experiential Learning: Experience as the Source of Learning and Development*. Prentice-Hall.

Kotera, Y., Richardson, M. & Sheffield, D. (2020). Effects of shinrin-yoku (forest bathing) and nature therapy on mental health: A systematic review and meta-analysis. *International Journal of Mental Health and Addiction*, 20: 337–361. https://doi.org/10.1007/s11469-020-00363-4

Kraft, R. J. & Sakofs, M., Eds. (1985). *The Theory of Experiential Education*. Association for Experiential Education.

Kulas, K. A. (2019). Developing an outdoor mindful activity-based curriculum for English language learners. School of Education Student Capstone Projects, Hamline University, Minnesota. https://digitalcommons.hamline.edu/hse_cp/285.

Lambert, M. (1992). Psychotherapy outcome research: Implications for integrative and eclectic therapists. In: J. C. Norcross & M. R. Goldfried (Eds.), *Handbook of Psychotherapy Integration* (pp. 94–129). Basic Books.

Lee, B. O. (2002). Chinese Indigenous psychotherapies in Singapore. *Counselling and Psychotherapy Research*, 2: 2–10. https://doi.org/10.1080/14733140212331384938.

Lehto, X. Y., Brown, S., Chen, Y. I. & Morrison, A. M. (2006). Yoga tourism as a niche within the wellness tourism market. *Tourism Recreation Research*, 31: 25–35. https://doi.org/10.1080/02508281.2006.11081244.

Leopold, A. (1949). *A Sand County Almanac*. Oxford University Press.

Lertzman, D. A. (2002). Rediscovering rites of passage: Education, transformation, and the transition to sustainability. *Conservation Ecology*, 5(2): 30. www.jstor.org/stable/26271823.

Lertzman, R. (2015). *Environmental Melancholia: Psychoanalytic Dimensions of Engagement*. Routledge.

Lewis, C. S. (1960). *Studies in Words*. Cambridge University Press.

Li, Q. (2018). *Forest Bathing: How Trees Can Help You Find Health and Happiness*. Viking.

Lovelock, J. E. (1972). Gaia as seen through the atmosphere. *Atmospheric Environment* (1967), 6: 579–580. https://doi.org/10.1016/0004-6981(72)90076-5.

Lymeus, F., Ahrling, M., Apelman, J., Florin, C. D. M., Nilsson, C., Vincenti, J., Zetterberg, A., Lindberg, P. & Hartig, T. (2020). Mindfulness-based restoration skills training (ReST) in a natural setting compared to conventional mindfulness training: Psychological functioning after a five-week course. *Frontiers in Psychology*, 11: 1560. https://doi.org/10.3389/fpsyg.2020.01560.

Macy, J. R. (1983). *Despair and Personal Power in the Nuclear Age*. New Society.

Markwell, N. & Gladwin, T. E. (2020). Shinrin-yoku (forest bathing) reduces stress and increases people's positive affect and well-being in comparison with its digital counterpart. *Ecopsychology*, 12: 247–256. https://doi.org/10.1089/eco.2019.0071.

Marx, K. (1888). Theses on Feuerbach. In: L. Colletti (ed), *Karl Marx: Early Writings* (G. Benton, trans.). Penguin (reprinted 1975).

Matapo, J. (2021). Mobilising Pacific Indigenous knowledges to reconceptualise a sustainable future: A Pasifika early childhood education perspective. *Asia-Pacific Journal of Research in Early Childhood Education*, 15: 45–63. www.pecerajournal.com/detail/30003285.

Matapo, J. & Baice, T. (2020). The art of wayfinding Pasifika success. *MAI Journal*, 9: 26–37. https://doi.org/10.20507/MAIJournal.2020.9.1.4.

Matapo, J. & Enari, D. (2021). Re-imagining the dialogic spaces of talanoa through Samoan onto-epistemology. *Waikato Journal of Education*, 26: 79–88. https://doi.org/10.15663/wje.v26i1.770.

Mikahere-Hall, A., Morice, M. P. & Pye, C. (2019). Waka Oranga: The development of an Indigenous professional organisation within a psychotherapeutic discourse in Aotearoa New Zealand. *Ata: Journal of Psychotherapy Aotearoa New Zealand*, 23: 23–34. https://doi.org/10.9791/ajpanz.2019.04.

MIND. (2007). *Ecotherapy: The Green Agenda for Mental Health.* www.bl.uk/collection-items/ecotherapy-the-green-agenda-for-mental-health.

Mohatt, G. V. (2010). Moving toward an Indigenous psychotherapy. *The Counselling Psychologist*, 38: 236–242. https://doi.org/10.1177/0011000009345532.

Morita, E., Fukuda, S., Nagano, J., Hamajima, N., Yamamoto, H., Iwai, Y., Nakashima, T., Ohira, H. & Shirakawa, T. J. P. H. (2007). Psychological effects of forest environments on healthy adults:

Shinrin-yoku (forest-air bathing, walking) as a possible method of stress reduction. *Public Health*, 121: 54–63. https://doi.org/10.1016/j.puhe.2006.05.024.

Morreira, S., Luckett, K., Kumala, S. H. & Ramgotra, M., Eds. (2021). *Decolonising Curricula and Pedagogy in Higher Education: Bringing Decolonial Theory into Contact With Teaching Practice*. Routledge.

Moylan, C. (2009). Treating depression: Towards an Indigenous psychotherapy. Doctoral dissertation, James Cook University, Australia. https://researchonline.jcu.edu.au/10578.

Murdoch, I. (1970). *The Sovereignty of Good*. Routledge & Kegan Paul.

Mwiti, G. (2014). African Indigenous psychotherapy. *Journal of Psychology & Christianity*, 33: 171–178. www.proquest.com/docview/1554575542.

Næss, A. (1973). The shallow and the deep, long-range ecology movement. A summary. *Inquiry*, 16: 95–100. https://doi.org/10.1080/00201747308601682.

Næss, A. (1975). Freedom, emotion, and self-subsistence. In: H. Glasser & A. R. Drengson (Eds.), *The Selected Works of Arne Næss*. Springer (reprinted 2005).

Næss, A. (1989). Ecosophy and Gestalt ontology. *The Trumpeter*, 6: 134–137. https://trumpeter.athabascau.ca/index.php/trumpet/article/view/756.

Næss, A. (1993). Intrinsic value: Will the defenders of nature please rise. In: P. Reed & D. Rothenberg (Eds.), *Wisdom in the Open Air* (pp. 70–82). University of Minnesota Press.

Næss, A. (1995). Self-realisation: An ecological approach to being in the world. In: G. Sessions (ed), *Deep Ecology for the 21st Century: Readings on the Philosophy of the New Environmentalism* (pp. 225–239). Shambala.

Næss, A. (2005). Deep ecology of wisdom: Explorations in unities of nature and cultures. In: H. Glasser & A. R. Drengson (Eds.), *The Selected Works of Arne Næss*. Springer.

Nagendra, H. R. (2013). Integrated yoga therapy for mental illness. *Indian Journal of Psychiatry*, 55: S337–339. www.ncbi.nlm.nih.gov/pmc/articles/PMC3768208.

Newcombe, S. (2009). The development of modern yoga: A survey of the field. *Religion Compass*, 3: 986–1002. https://doi.org/10.1111/j.1749-8171.2009.00171.x.

Newes, S. & Bandoroff, S. (2004). What is adventure therapy. In: S. Newes & S. Bandoroff (Eds.), *Coming of Age: The Evolving Field of Adventure Therapy* (pp. 1–30). Association for Experiential Education.

Norris, J. (2011). Crossing the threshold mindfully: Exploring rites of passage models in adventure therapy. *Journal of Adventure Education & Outdoor Learning*, 11: 109–126. https://doi.org/10.1080/14729679.2011.633380.

Norton, C. L. (2009). Ecopsychology and social work: Creating an interdisciplinary framework for redefining person-in-environment. *Ecopsychology*, 1: 138–145. https://doi.org/10.1089/eco.2009.0046.

Oh, K. H., Shin, W. S., Khil, T. G. & Kim, D. J. (2020). Six-step model of nature-based therapy process. *International Journal of Environmental Research and Public Health*, 17: 685. https://doi.org/10.3390/ijerph17030685.

Oles, G. W. (1995). 'Borrowing' activities from another culture: A Native American's perspective. In: K. Warren, M. Sakofs, & J. S. Hunt (Eds.), *The Theory of Experiential Education* (pp. 195–201). Kendall & Hunt.

Orians, G. H. (1986). An ecological and evolutionary approach to landscape aesthetics. In: E. C. Penning-Rowsell & D. Lowenthal (Eds.), *Landscape Meanings and Values* (pp. 3–25). Routledge.

Panov, V. (2017). From environmental psychology to subject-environment interactions. *Advances in Social Science, Education and Humanities Research*, 124: 1135–1139. https://doi.org/10.2991/iccessh-17.2017.265.

Peters, M. D., Godfrey, C. M., Khalil, H., McInerney, P., Parker, D. & Soares, C. B. (2015). Guidance for conducting systematic scoping reviews. *JBI Evidence Implementation*, 13: 141–146. https://doi.org/10.1097/XEB.0000000000000050.

Peterson, J., Pearce, P. F., Ferguson, L. A. & Langford, C. A. (2017). Understanding scoping reviews: Definition, purpose, and process. *Journal of the American Association of Nurse Practitioners*, 29: 12–16. https://doi.org/10.1002/2327-6924.12380.

Pham, M. T., Rajić, A., Greig, J. D., Sargeant, J. M., Papadopoulos, A. & McEwen, S. A. (2014). A scoping review of scoping reviews: Advancing the approach and enhancing the consistency. *Research Synthesis Methods*, 5: 371–85. https://doi.org/10.1002/jrsm.1123.

Potgieter, C. A. (2018). The lived body experience of the therapist-practitioner in the South African social service delivery field. Doctoral dissertation, North-West University, South Africa. https://dspace.nwu.ac.za/handle/10394/31184.

Priest, S. (2021). Adventure therapy in Canada. *Academia Letters*, Article 3831. https://doi.org/10.20935/AL3831.

Priestman, A. (2015). We the human animals: Exploring an embodied, relational and wild approach to therapy. *Self & Society*, 43: 138–147. https://doi.org/10.1080/03060497.2015.1054711.

Quinn, D. (1995). *Ishmael*. Bantam/Turner Book.

Rajoo, K. S., Karam, D. S. & Abdullah, M. Z. (2020). The physiological and psychosocial effects of forest therapy: A systematic review. *Urban Forestry & Urban Greening*, 54: 126744. https://doi.org/10.1016/j.ufug.2020.126744.

Relf, D. & Dorn, S. (1995). Horticulture: Meeting the needs of special populations. *Horticultural Technology*, 5: 94–103. https://doi.org/10.21273/HORTTECH.5.2.94.

Reser, J. P. (1995). Whither environmental psychology? The transpersonal ecopsychology crossroads. *Journal of Environmental Psychology*, 15: 235–257. https://doi.org/10.1016/0272-4944(95)90006-3.

Rivers, S., Rodgers, B., May, J. & Tudor, K. (2022). On – and in – bicultural encounter. *Person-Centred & Experiential Psychotherapy*, 21: 172–87. https://doi.org/10.1080/14779757.2022.2067782.

Robyn-Rapsey, F. (2013). *Made to Matter: White Fathers, Stolen Generations*. Sydney University Press.

Rogers, C. R. (1959). A theory of therapy, personality and interpersonal relationships, as developed in the client-centred framework. In: S. Koch (ed), *Psychology: A Study of a Science. Vol. 3: Formulation of the Person and the Social Context* (pp. 184–256). McGraw-Hill.

Rohnke, K. (1986). Project adventure: A widely used generic product. *Journal of Physical Education, Recreation & Dance*, 57: 68–69. https://doi.org/10.1080/07303084.1986.10606139.

Roszak, T. (1992). *The Voice of the Earth: An Exploration of Ecopsychology*. Red Wheel/Weiser (reprinted in 2001).

Roszak, T. E., Gomes, M. E. & Kanner, A. D. (1995). *Ecopsychology: Restoring the Earth, Healing the Mind*. Sierra Club Books.

Russell, K. C. (2001). What is wilderness therapy? *Journal of Experiential Education*, 24: 70–79. https://doi.org/10.1177/105382590102400203.

Russell, K. C. (2006). Brat camp, boot camp, or …? Exploring wilderness therapy program theory. *Journal of Adventure Education & Outdoor Learning*, 6: 51–67. https://doi.org/10.1080/14729670685200741.

Rust, M. -J. (2020). *Towards an Ecopsychotherapy*. Confer Books.

Sahlin, E., Matuszczyk, J. V., Ahlborg Jr, G. & Grahn, P. (2012). How do participants in nature-based therapy experience and evaluate their rehabilitation? *Journal of Therapeutic Horticulture*, 22: 8–23. www.jstor.org/stable/pdf/24865211.pdf.

Said, E. (1978). *Orientalism*. Pantheon Books.

Schell-Faucon, S. (2001). *Journey into the Inner Self and Encounter with the Other: Transformation Trails with Militarised Youth of Katorus*. http://csvr.org.za/docs/youth/journeyintoinner.pdf.

Schouten, J. W. (1991). Personal rites of passage and the reconstruction of self. In: R. H. Holman & M. R. Solomon (Eds.), *Advances in Consumer Research,* Volume 18 (pp. 49–51). Association for Consumer Research.

Shaw, M. (2021). *Smoke Hole – Looking to the Wild in the Time of the Spyglass*. Chelsea Green.

Segal, D., Harper, N. J. & Rose, K. (2020). Nature-based therapy. In: N. J. Harper & W. W. Dobud (Eds.), *Outdoor Therapies: An Introduction to Practices, Possibilities, and Critical Perspectives* (pp. 95–107). Routledge.

Shepard, P. (1982). *Nature and Madness*. Sierra Club Books.

Shepherd, T. & Woodard, W. (2012). 'Not home' is sometimes where we start. *Ata: Journal of Psychotherapy Aotearoa New Zealand*, 16: 51–71. https://doi.org/10.9791/ajpanz.2012.07.

Shoemaker, C. A. (2002). The profession of horticultural therapy compared with other allied therapies. *Journal of*

Therapeutic Horticulture, 13: 74–81. https://doi.org/10.17660/ActaHortic.2004.639.21.

Shweder, R. A. (1990). Cultural psychology – What is it? In: J. W. Stigler, R. A. Shweder & G. Herdt (Eds.), *Cultural Psychology* (pp. 27–66). Cambridge University Press.

Singh, M. (2018). The cultural evolution of shamanism. *Behavioral and Brain Sciences*, 41: e66. https://doi.org/10.1017/S0140525X17001893.

Singleton, M. (2010). *Yoga Body: The Origins of Modern Posture Practice*. Oxford University Press.

Smith, L. T. (1999). *Decolonizing Methodologies: Research and Indigenous Peoples*. Zed Books.

Snyder, G. (2010). *The Practice of the Wild*. Counterpoint Press.

Söderback, I., Söderström, M. & Schälander, E. (2004). Horticultural therapy: The 'healing garden' and gardening in rehabilitation measures at Danderyd Hospital Rehabilitation Clinic, Sweden. *Pediatric Rehabilitation*, 7: 245–260. https://doi.org/10.1080/13638490410001711416.

Song, C., Ikei, H. & Miyazaki, Y. (2016). Physiological effects of nature therapy: A review of the research in Japan. *International Journal of Environmental Research and Public Health*, 13: 781. https://doi.org/10.3390/ijerph13080781.

Soto, J. A. (2008). *Marine Therapy: Health Benefits of Seawater Minerals*. AuthorHouse.

Spivak, G. C. (1988). Can the subaltern speak? In: C. Nelson & L. Grossberg (Eds.), *Marxism and the Interpretation of Culture* (pp. 271–313). Macmillan.

Stigsdotter, U. K., Palsdottir, A. M., Burls, A., Chermaz, A., Ferrini, F. & Grahn, P. (2011). Nature-based therapeutic interventions. In: K.

Nilsson, M. Sangster, C. Gallis, T. Hartig, S. de Vries, K. Seeland, & J. Schipperijn (Eds.), *Forests, Trees and Human Health* (pp. 309–342). Springer.

Stone, C. D. (1972). Should trees have standing? Towards legal rights for natural objects. *Southern California Law Review*, 45: 450–501. https://ir.law.fsu.edu/cgi/viewcontent.cgi?article=1753&context=lr.

Sue, S. (2003). In defense of cultural competency in psychotherapy and treatment. *American Psychologist*, 58: 964. https://doi.org/10.1037/0003-066X.58.11.964.

Sue, S. & Zane, N. (1987). The role of culture and cultural techniques in psychotherapy: A critique and reformulation. *American Psychologist*, 42: 37. https://doi.org/10.1037/0003-066X.42.1.37.

Sue, S., Zane, N., Nagayama Hall, G. C. & Berger, L. K. (2009). The case for cultural competency in psychotherapeutic interventions. *Annual Review of Psychology*, 60: 525–548. https://doi.org/10.1146/annurev.psych.60.110707.163651.

Taylor, J. & Kukutai, T. (2016). *Indigenous Data Sovereignty: Toward an Agenda*. ANU Press & Centre for Aboriginal Economic Policy Research.

Totton, N. (2011). *Wild Therapy: Undomesticating Inner and Outer Worlds*. PCCS Books.

Totton, N. (2013). The practice of wild therapy. *Therapy Today*, 25(5). www.bacp.co.uk/bacp-journals/therapy-today/2014/june-2014/the-practice-of-wild-therapy.

Tsunetsugu, Y., Park, B. J. & Miyazaki, Y. (2010). Trends in research related to 'Shinrin-yoku' (taking in the forest atmosphere or forest bathing) in Japan. *Environmental Health and Preventive Medicine*, 15: 27–37. https://doi.org/10.1007/s12199-009-0091-z.

Tudor, K. (2011). Understanding empathy. *Transactional Analysis*

Journal, 41: 39–57. https://doi.org/10.1177/036215371104100107.

Tudor, K. & Worrall, M. (2006). *Person-Centred Therapy: A Clinical Philosophy*. Routledge.

Tui Atua, T. T. T. E. (2014). Whispers and vanities in Samoan Indigenous religious culture. In: T. M. Suaalii-Sauni, M. A. Wendt, V. Mo'a, N. Fuamatu, U. L. Vaai, R. Whaitiri & S. L. Filipo (Eds.), *Whispers and Vanities, Samoan Indigenous Knowledge and Religion* (pp. 11–42). Huia.

Turner, V. (1987). Betwixt and between: The liminal period in rites of passage. In: L. C. Mahdi, S. Foster, & M. Little (Eds.), *Betwixt and Between: Patterns of Masculine and Feminine Initiation* (pp. 3–19). Open Court.

Turner, V., Abrahams, R. D. & Harris, A. (1969). *The Ritual Process: Structure and Anti-Structure*. Taylor & Francis.

Ungar, M., Dumond, C. & Mcdonald, W. (2005). Risk, resilience, and outdoor programmes for at-risk children. *Journal of Social Work*, 5: 319–338. https://doi.org/10.1177/1468017305058938.

United States Wilderness Act 1964. Public law 99-577. Statutes at large 78 Stat. 890.

Usher, K., Durkin, J. & Bhullar, N. (2019). Eco-anxiety: How thinking about climate change-related environmental decline is affecting our mental health. *International Journal of Mental Health Nursing*, 28: 1233–1234. https://doi.org/10.1111/inm.12673.

Van Gennep, A. (2019). *The Rites of Passage*. University of Chicago Press.

Verzwyvelt, L. A., McNamara, A., Xu, X. & Stubbins, R. (2021). Effects of virtual reality v. biophilic environments on pain and distress in oncology patients: A case-crossover pilot study. *Scientific Reports*, 11: 20196. https://doi.org/10.1038/s41598-021-99763-2.

von Eckartsberg, R. (1979). The eco-psychology of personal culture building: An existential-hermeneutic approach. In: A. Giorgi, W. F. Fischer & R. von Eckartsberg (Eds.), *Duquesne Studies in Phenomenological Psychology,* Vol. 3 (pp. 227–244). Humanities Press.

Walsh, R. (1989). What is a shaman? Definition, origin and distribution. *Journal of Transpersonal Psychology*, 21: 1–11. www.atpweb.org/jtparchive/trps-21-89-01-001.pdf.

White, M. P., Pahl, S., Wheeler, B. W., Fleming, L. E. F. & Depledge, M. H. (2016). The blue gym: What can blue space do for you and what can you do for blue space? *Journal of the Marine Biological Association of the United Kingdom*, 96: 5–12. https://doi.org/10.1017/S0025315415002209.

Wild Mindfulness. (2022). *Wild Mindfulness Australia*. www.wildmindfulness.com.au.

Wilson, N. W., Ross, M. K., Lafferty, K. & Jones, R. (2008). A review of ecotherapy as an adjunct form of treatment for those who use mental health services. *Journal of Public Mental Health*, 7(3): 23–35. https://doi.org/10.1108/17465729200800020.

Wolsko, C. & Hoyt, K. (2012). Employing the restorative capacity of nature: Pathways to practicing ecotherapy among mental health professionals. *Ecopsychology*, 4: 10–24. https://doi.org/10.1089/eco.2012.0002.

Yang, K. S. (2000). Monocultural and cross-cultural Indigenous approaches: The royal road to the development of a balanced global psychology. *Asian Journal of Social Psychology*, 3: 241–263. https://doi.org/10.1111/1467-839X.00067.

Zak, A. (2020). *Incorporating Yoga and Mindfulness for Kids into Outdoor Programs: Resource for Environmental Educators*. Sun and Moon Yoga 200-hour Foundations Program. http://docplayer.net/221840767-Sun-and-moon-yoga-200-hour-foundations-program-final-project-yoga-teaching-product.html.

INDEX

Karnac Books, founded in 1950 and relaunched in 2020, publishes seminal and contemporary texts on psychotherapy and psychoanalysis. It continues its long tradition of exploring the intricacies of these disciplines, providing space for the best writers on the complexities of the mind.